WARRIOR
The First and The Last

JOHN WINTON

MARITIME BOOKS

Contents

	Page
Chapter 1: First Commission	3
Chapter 2: Life in the Victorian Navy	13
Chapter 3: A Day on Board *Warrior*	24
Chapter 4: Decline and Decay	36
Chapter 5: New Life	47
Principal Dates in *Warrior's* History	83
Senior Officers	85
Establishment on Commissioning	86
Daily Routines on board	88
Sources	92
Index	94

First published in Great Britain by
Maritime Books, Liskeard, Cornwall.

© *John Winton 1987*

ISBN 0 907771 34 3

Typeset and printed in Great Britain by
Penwell Ltd., Parkwood, Callington, Cornwall.

Front cover: W. Sartori
Back cover: L/Air (Phot) A. Reid

1

First Commission

'The black snake amongst the rabbits', or 'the raven amongst the daws', old-time sailors used to call *Warrior*, when they compared her long low black shape to the stubby chequered sides of her contemporaries. She was the most revolutionary warship of her time—perhaps even the most revolutionary warship of all time. *Warrior* was the largest, fastest, most powerful warship of her day. She made everything else obsolete overnight. As Admiral Ballard once wrote, when *Warrior* left the slipway 'all war values had to be reckoned on a perfectly clean slate'.

Warrior was by no means the first ironclad in the Royal Navy, and the original design concept was that she should be a frigate. Nevertheless, as built, *Warrior* was certainly the first ocean-going, iron-hulled *battleship*, in anything like the modern sense of that word. Ironically, she is also the last. All the rest of the 150 or so of her successors which have worn the White Ensign have long gone down to enemy action, or to the breakers' yard. Because her stout, almost rust-proof, wrought iron hull happened to remain useful to the Navy until 1979, *Warrior* alone survives.

The first impulse to build *Warrior* certainly did not come from the Admiralty. As the superior naval power in the world, Great Britain did not need to innovate. 'Newfangled' inventions were the province of weaker nations, who had to try and make up in ingenuity for what they lacked in sheer brute naval strength. Even when an innovation was successful, Great Britain had the industrial resources quickly to outstrip the original innovator.

The pressure to build a British ironclad arose from one of the periodical 'invasion scares' which swept through Victorian England from time to time. Towards the end of the 1850s relations with France, always prickly, deteriorated sharply. The Emperor Napoleon III was keen to emulate and even to surpass the military prowess of his famous namesake. Anti-British feeling in France was fanned in 1858 when the Orsini plot to assassinate Napoleon III failed and the Italian conspirators took refuge in England.

On 1 January 1857, the ship designer and naval constructor Dupuy de Lôme had been appointed Directeur du Material in France. De Lôme had revolutionary ideas about warship construction. He stopped the building of any more of the old wooden-walled ships of the line and instead produced his own designs for a new French fleet,

in which the ships would all be iron-hulled. The first six ships of the new fleet were ordered in March 1858. Their names were to be *Gloire*, *Invincible*, *Normandie*, *Couronne*, *Magenta* and *Solferino*. But French industrial capacity was not yet capable of producing such ships. The first three were therefore literally 'ironclads'—wooden ships clad with wrought iron plates overlaid on their sides. The first of these was *Gloire*.

Gloire was 256 feet long, displaced 5618 tons, had a complement of about 550 officers and men, an armament of 34 guns on the main deck and two on the upper deck, and a top speed of 13 knots. According to *The Times*, some said *Gloire* was 'the most perfect and most formidable vessel ever built', others that she was 'neither the one nor the other, but a bad and irremediable failure'. As *The Times* said, the truth lay between these two extremes, but clearly she was going to be an unusual warship, and an advance on any other man-of-war of the day. She was ordered on 4 March 1858, launched on 24 November 1859, and completed in August 1860. But rumours, press stories and intelligence reports about the new warship had reached England long before she was ready for sea.

French belligerence was in any case no secret. Queen Victoria and Prince Albert visited Cherbourg in August 1858, for a visit which was intended to repair Anglo-French relations. But on every side the Royal couple saw evidence of new fortications, a fleet of new ships and a general air of expectancy and preparation for war. 'The war preparations of the French are immense', said Albert, 'ours despicable. Our Ministers use fine phrases, but they do nothing. My blood boils within me!'

Prince Albert's was not the only blood to boil. At home there was a vociferous press and parliamentary campaign, putting pressure on the Admiralty to restore national prestige and safeguard the country from an invasion of frogs.

The first Admiralty proposal was simply to follow the French and place iron plates on the side of a wooden vessel. But, fortunately for the Navy and the country, the First Lord of the Admiralty, Sir John Pakington, took up a much bolder idea, proposed by Captain Sir Baldwin Walker, the Surveyor of the Navy, for an iron-hulled ship, to the broad design of the Chief Constructor Isaac Watts and with the assistance of the ship designer John Scott Russell.

The specification was for a frigate, with 4" of iron

The French Gloire **the first ironclad . . .**

protection on her sides extending from the upper deck to five feet below the waterline, over a length of 200 feet amidships, with protected bulkheads at each end, so as to form the middle of the ship into an armoured box or 'citadel'. The bow and stern sections were to be un-armoured, but sub-divided into watertight compartments. The hull would have 34 gun ports on the main deck, the ports to be at least nine feet above the waterline in the midships section, with two upper deck guns as bow and stern chasers. The top speed was to be 13½ knots. Under sail, the ship would be rigged as for an 80-gun ship.

It was an historic decision and, once it was taken, the Admiralty lost no time putting it into effect. To have as many alternatives to Watts' basic design as possible, Royal Dockyards and private firms were invited to submit designs, and fourteen did so, although they were all rejected in the end, in favour of the Admiralty Office's own design.

Tenders for the new warship were called for on 29 April 1859. The order to build the ship under contract, at £31 10s. per ton B.O.M., was placed with the Thames Iron-works (formerly C.J. Mare & Co.) of Blackwall on 11 May. The first keel-plate was laid down on 25 May, at the Thames Ironworks slipway on the left bank of Bow Creek, where it flowed into the Thames. John Penn & Sons, Greenwich, tendered to build the engines, boilers and the propellor hoisting gear on 16 May and their tender was accepted on 25th.

The ship was to be launched in eleven months and completed for sea three months later, the specified delivery date being 11 July 1860 (which would have been before *Gloire*). She was named *Warrior* on 5 October 1859. The contract for a sister ship was placed with Napiers of Glasgow the same month. She was to be called *Invincible*, a name later changed to *Black Prince.*

Any ship as new and revolutionary as *Warrior* was bound to attract die-hard criticism. 'This miserable, peg-topped, leangutted model,' said Admiral Sir Edward Belcher, speaking for the older generation. *The Times* in January 1860 had rather more rational criticism, in a letter signed 'Common Sense' pointing out the vulnerability of *Warrior*'s unarmoured ends.

Warrior's **designer, John Scott Russell c1860.**

4

Nevertheless, *Warrior* was the first ship to incorporate four of the great Victorian advances in warship building: armour protection; an iron structure in both frame and plating; a ratio of length to beam of 6.5 to 1; and a system of subdivision in her compartments (92 in all) to give much improved watertight integrity. As completed, she displaced 9,210 tons (hull 6,150 tons, equipment 3,060), with an overall length of 420 feet (380 feet between perpendiculars), a beam of 58¼ feet and a draught of 26 feet. She cost about £390,000, including the guns and 850 tons of coal.

Because of changes in the design and the specifications (what would nowadays be called 'the MoD moving the goalposts') *Warrior* was not built to the contracted deadline which, in any case, was unrealistic. But the Admiralty accepted the delay, waived the penalty clause in the contract for £50,000 if the delivery date was not met, and even paid the Thames Ironworks' claim for an extra £44,503 above the contract price (which saved the firm from going into liquidation).

would bear'. A heavy gun was discharged on the upper deck, to try and shift her by its concussion, but she still stuck fast.

It was 2.30pm, high tide, and if the ship were not launched soon, in a few minutes, the tide would begin to fall and she could not be launched until the next spring tide. A hawser was made fast to a tug in the river. Hundreds of workmen pounded the slipway with hammers, while the men on board ran from side to side. But still she would not budge. At last, at about 3pm (half an hour late) when two more tugs had been brought up, *Warrior* began to move, an eye-witness said, 'very slowly—so slowly that her motion was scarcely perceptible. From that time she never wholly stopped—as the reporters from the newspapers (including *The Times*) pardonably state—but minute after minute continued to descend. After a while a steam tug or two took hold of her, and as soon as she began to move off with a promising degree of speed, Sir John Pakington dashed a bottle of wine on her bows, with a

The great "steam-frigate" Warrior on the slip at the Thomas Iron Works Blackwall.

Warrior, 'this formidable iron-cased frigate', as *The Times* said, 'the largest man-of-war ever built, and more than 1,600 tons larger than the largest vessel in the world after the *Great Eastern*', was eventually launched by Sir John Pakington on Saturday 29 December 1860—the first time, it was said, since the launch of the *Thunderer* (in 1831) that this ceremony had not been performed by a lady. It was a bitterly cold day, with thick snow on the ground, but in spite of the weather the shipyard was crowded with some hundreds of people who were present to see 'the first start of this invulnerable frigate'.

At first it seemed that *Warrior* would disappoint them. The 'dog-shores' were knocked away, but hard frost overnight had frozen the grease on the slipway and the ship could not move. Hydraulic presses, kept for just such an emergency, were 'worked and pumped to the utmost they

"God speed the Warrior", and the noble ship ran off as easily and gracefully as any yacht ever took the tide . . .'

After the launch, *Warrior* was secured to buoys off the East India Dock for the night. Next day, 30 December, she was moved to the Victoria Dock, a quarter of a mile down river from the Thames Ironworks, for fitting out.

At her launch, *Warrior* had only 30 armour plates fitted, one row of 15 on each side, the rest being put in position when she was fitted out in the Victoria Dock. The armour plate was made at the Thames Ironworks, from best scrap iron repeatedly hammered, and then rolled. The plates were 4½" thick, mainly 15 feet by three in area, and each weighed about 4 tons. They were tongued and grooved together and secured in place by seventeen 1¼" diameter bolts screwed inside the hull between the ship's frames. One square foot of armour, including the teak backing,

The first known photograph . . . fitting out at Greenhithe 1861.

weighed 284 lbs. About 950 tons of armour plates were made for the ship and the total weight of armour and backing was 1,354 tons.

The teak backing, 18″ thick, was in two layers, the outer laid vertically, the inner horizontally. The armour and backing had a vertical height of 22 feet, of which about 16 feet was above the waterline and six feet below. It extended along the central section of the ship's sides for a length of 123 feet and was carried across the width of the ship to form an armoured box or 'citadel'. The athwartships armour, which enclosed the two ends of the 'citadel', was wrought iron 4″ thick, with 12″ of teak backing. The last eighty or so feet at bow and stern were unarmoured and, as there was no such thing at that time as long range 'plunging fire', the decks were also unarmoured, but the length of the upper deck was enclosed by stout bulwarks, seven feet high.

The majority of the guns were mounted on the main deck, within the armoured citadel. Originally it was planned to have forty 68-pounder Muzzle Loading Smooth Bores (MLSBs) but this was one of the many plans changed more than once during building. When first commissioned, *Warrior* had two 68-pdr. MLSBs forward of the citadel, and two aft of it, on each side. Within the citadel

were (from forward to aft on each side) four 68-pdr MLSBs, four 110-pdr Breech Loading Rifled (BLR) guns, and another five 68-pdr MLSBs. This gave a main deck broadside of 17 guns a side—34 guns in all. On the upper deck were two 110-pdr BLR chasers, one forward and one aft. Also on the upper deck were four 40-pdr BLRs (the ship was originally to have had 70-pdrs, but none were available). The total armament was therefore 40 guns and *Warrior* was first officially designated as a 40-gun Screw Ship, Iron.

The ship commissioned in Victoria Dock from Woolwich Yard on 1 August 1861. Her first commanding officer was Captain The Hon. Arthur Auckland Leopold Pedro Cochrane, CB, third son of the famous Admiral Cochrane, 10th Earl of Dundonald, hero of the Napoleonic Wars. The christian names Leopold Pedro were a reminder that when he was born in 1824 his father was in the service of Don Pedro, Emperor of Brazil. Captain Cochrane had been present at the bombardment of Acre in 1840, and had seen action in the Fatshan Creek in China in 1857.

As with new 'first of class' warships to this day, *Warrior*'s wardroom had a hand-picked look about it. The Commander, and Second in Command, was George Tryon, one of the ablest naval officers of his generation, who later rose to be Vice Admiral and C-in-C Mediterranean, only to lose his life tragically through his own error when his flagship *Victoria* was rammed and sunk by *Camperdown* off the coast of the Lebanon in June 1893. Her Gunnery Lieutenant, who joined in March 1863, was Jackie Fisher, the future Admiral of the Fleet and First Sea Lord. Her complement on first commissioning, as given in the Ship's Book, was 51 officers, 83 petty officers, 382 seamen, stokers and idlers, 63 boys, and 125 Royal Marines.

But *Warrior*, like all the early ironclads, suffered from a shortage of men, because a conservative Admiralty refused to acknowledge that ironclads needed new manning scales. From time immemorial, warships had been graded in 'rates', according to the number of guns they carried and their complements were rigidly fixed, being assessed on the watch and quarter bill of a ship of that rate.

But 'rates' did not apply to ironclads. Simply to count the number of guns, as in the old days, was absurd. That would put *Warrior*, undoubtedly the most powerful warship afloat, down among the frigates. But Admiralty bureaucrats, then as now, stuck rigidly to their rules. *Warrior* had 40 guns. Therefore she must be a frigate. However, the Gunnery Branch had calculated that *Warrior* needed 740 men, which was close to the number in a third-rate ship of the line, which was 705. Therefore *Warrior*, for manning purposes, was classed as a third-rate, with a complement of 705 men.

Warrior left Victoria Dock still unfinished (because the depth of water there was not enough for any more weight to be added to her) and moved to Greenhithe on 8 August to complete her fitting out. On 9 September she sailed for Spithead and, after a docking in Portsmouth, began to carry out her trials.

The first Commanding Officer—Captain The Hon. Arthur Cochrane.

Warrior's engines, with a nominal horsepower of 1,250, were jet-condensing, horizontal-trunk, single expansion engines, with a piston stroke of four feet. The cylinder bore was 9 feet 4" (the largest in diameter ever cast for a marine steam engine). Full Speed was 55 shaft revolutions per minute, with a piston speed of about 5 mph. The ship had ten rectangular multi-tubular (440 brass tubes per boiler) fire-tube wrought iron boilers, four in the forward and six in the after boiler room. Each boiler had four furnaces, contained 29 tons of water, and was 14 feet long, by

ILLUSTRATED LONDON NEWS—10 AUGUST 1861.

Underway at last.

Moored in the Hamoaze Plymouth c1862.

10 feet 3″ wide, and 12 feet 4″ high. Normal steam pressure was 20-22 psi.

The official speed trials took place over the measured mile in Stokes Bay, near Portsmouth, on 17 October. The ship had 760 tons of Nixon's navigation coal, four month's provisions under hatches and all her sea stores on board, and she drew 26 feet 5 inches aft and 25 feet 6 inches forward. Sir John Pakington and Thomas Lloyd, Engineer-in-Chief to the Admiralty, had both embarked for the occasion and saw *Warrior* do six runs for a true mean speed of 14.354 knots. The highest speed recorded on one run was 16.514 knots, with the tide—a record-breaking run during which the boiler steam pressure rose to 24.3 psi and the stokehold temperature in the after boiler room soared to 129°F.

After the trials were over, Captain Cochrane entertained Sir John Pakington and the other guests to lunch. When ''The Queen'' and the usual loyal toasts had been given, Captain Cochrane proposed 'the health of Sir John Pakington and success to the *Warrior*'. In reply, Sir John, who had once said 'I often wonder how I mustered sufficient courage to order the construction of such a novel vessel' (to which Mare the builder is supposed to have replied '*I* often wonder how *I* mustered sufficient courage to undertake it') now said that this was one of the most grati-

fying days of his life. He had been anxious to see the *Warrior* in her sea-going condition, and what he had seen that day had far exceeded his warmest expectations.

Warrior could officially do 14.3 knots under steam, 13 knots under sail. She once logged 17.7 knots under both. At full power she consumed about 11 tons of coal an hour, so that her bunker capacity of 850 tons was theoretically enough for 77 hours, or about 1,100 miles, at full speed. But at the normal 5-6 knots cruising speeds of Victorian fleets, her endurance would be well over 2,000 miles.

Warrior was accepted into service on 24 October 1861. On 30th, she sailed to Portland where, next day, she was inspected by Rear Admiral Robert Smart, commanding the Channel Squadron in which *Warrior* was now to serve. That same afternoon *Warrior* sailed on her first extended sea voyage, to Queenstown, Cork, in southern Ireland, in company with Smart's flagship, the 91-gun screw ship of the line *Revenge*.

Revenge was not much older than *Warrior*, having been launched only in 1859 and completed the following year. But compared with *Warrior*'s long low black hull, *Revenge*'s high wooden black-and-white chequered sides, with their pronounced 'tumble-home', and her double row of gunports, had an antique look about them, reminiscent of the ships of Nelson's day.

Warrior made everything look antique. It seemed that the whole country, even those who knew almost nothing about the Navy, realised that here was the ship, and the shape, of the future. Everybody wanted to see *Warrior*. On 10 January 1862, at Cowes, the Prince of Wales and the Prince of Hesse came on board, with their suites. In February, *Warrior* sailed with the Squadron to Lisbon and to Gibraltar. At Lisbon, the Russian, Austrian, Swedish, Spanish, Italian, Dutch, Prussian, Danish and Belgian ambassadors all crowded onboard and were duly saluted, with national honours and anthems, on leaving. The next day, the King of Portugal himself came on board and was shown round the ship.

At sea, under the critical eyes of Admiral Smart and the rest of the Channel Squadron, *Warrior* performed very well. Because of her length and the thickness of her armoured sides, she had a rather stiff, slow motion which sailors used to wooden ships found strange at first. Under steam, she was consistently a knot or two faster than her sister *Black Prince* and could leave the rest out of sight; in a competitive trial on 15 November 1861, during her first cruise with *Revenge, Warrior* logged 16.3 knots while the best the flagship could do was 11.

Under sail, she went well enough with the wind abeam but it was found difficult to put her about from one tack to the other. Her log records that, in moderately smooth water, under all plain sail, she tacked in 6 minutes 40 seconds. Swinging the cross-jack yard when the helm was put down reduced the time to 5 minutes 20 seconds. Because of her length, she tended to hang 'in irons', with her bows pointing up into the wind and her sails flapping idly.

Wearing, that is, changing course with the wind crossing the stern from one quarter to the other, took very much longer than tacking. On 1 December 1862, with a Force 3 wind, wearing took as long as 48 minutes. But on 30 January 1863, wind Force 5-6 and a moderate sea on the weather bow, under first reef of topsails, foresail, jib and fore trysail, wearing took only 16 minutes.

In moderate gales, *Warrior* sailed remarkably well, considering the small amount of sail she spread for her tonnage. Her 17 knots, steaming and sailing, has never been surpassed. With six men on the wheel and eight on the relieving tackles on the rudder yoke-head, the helm could be put over in 1½ minutes. Her one serious drawback was that she was undoubtedly very bow heavy, plunging her bows deep into head seas, and shipping water green over her upper deck forward in quite moderate sea states.

Warrior spent from early March to early June 1862 in Devonport where alterations and improvements, mainly to try and remedy her bow-heaviness, were carried out by the dockyard. Her bowsprit was shortened and lightened. The cat-heads for the two bower anchors were moved, so that the weight of the anchors was further aft. The sailors' heads (latrines) up forward in the bows, which had often been unusable at sea, were repositioned amidships. The maindeck gun ports were fitted with vulcanized rubber linings on their inner edges to make them watertight. There were some other additions: two new and much

stronger capstans, one of iron and the other of wood, six more Downton pumps for pumping out bilges, and two towing bollards on the quarterdeck. Also fitted in 1863 was a type of gas lighting, in the engine room and screw alley, with twelve burners which gave a brilliant light compared with the old oil lamps. The gas was actually manufactured on board by burning oil in a 'retort' and storing the resultant gas in a gasometer on the upper deck.

Warrior sailed, on 10 June, for Queenstown, and during the year visited Portland, Lisbon and Gibraltar again. In August, she escorted the Royal Yacht *Osborne* for a cruise in Portland Roads. Her officers of the watch and gangway staff must soon have become blasé about royal visitors. HRH Prince Arthur, the Prince and Princess of Hesse, the Viceroy of Egypt, the Crown Prince of Russia, Prince Napoleon, the Prince of Saxe Weimar, Prince Adalbert of Prussia (arriving in the Prussian frigate *Gazelle*) and the Prince of Italy, all visited the ship during the year. The Prince of Wales paid two visits and HRH Prince Alfred, Queen Victoria's second son 'Affie', who was then an 18 year old Midshipman destined for a naval career, came three times.

In March 1863, there was yet another royal occasion, when *Warrior*, with *Revenge* (flag), *Defence* and *Resistance* met the Royal Yacht bringing Princess Alexandra of Denmark, the Prince of Wales' intended bride, from Antwerp, and escorted her to Gravesend. ('Well done,' was the signal from the Royal Yacht, 'Princess is pleased'.) Such was the pace of naval building in the 1860s that *Defence* and *Resistance*, known as 'steam rams' because of their ploughshare-shaped bows, were both brand new iron-hulled battleships, even newer than *Warrior* herself, having been laid down a few months after her. The 'Black Fleet' of the 1860s and 1870s, so-called because of the colour of their hulls, was already emerging.

As 'first of class', *Warrior* was always being modified and re-equipped, with constant alterations and additions. She was docked frequently—twelve times in ten years—an average of about every ten months. From March to June 1863, she was again in Devonport making good defects, and having new gear, in this case hydraulic steering gear, fitted for trials. At the end of June, she again went into dry dock at Portsmouth (where Affie visited her for the fourth time).

Warrior came out of dock at the beginning of July and on 11th weighed anchor and sailed from Spithead with the Channel Squadron for a Round Britain cruise. The composition of the squadron showed the Navy, as always, in a state of transition, with both wooden and iron-hulled ships. The flagship *Edgar*, wearing the flag of Rear Admiral Sydney Colpoys Dacres CB, was a 91-gun wooden screw battleship launched in 1858. With *Warrior* were four more of the Black Fleet: her sister ship *Black Prince*, *Defence*, *Resistance* and *Royal Oak*, which had originally been designed as a wooden ship but had been converted during building, with her hull lengthened and cladded with iron plates, her armament changed and her gundecks reduced from two to one. Thus the six battle-

A fine lithograph by T.G. Dalton, published in 1861.

ships taking part in the cruise were of four different classes of ship. Also on the cruise were two wooden frigates, *Emerald* and *Liverpool*, and the despatch vessel *Trinculo*.

The main object of the cruise was, of course, publicity for the Navy. As Geoffrey Phipps Hornby, *Edgar*'s flag captain, wrote to his wife, 'We are doing popularity to a great extent. Ostensibly we are to show the ships and what happy fellows the British mariners are in a man-of-war—nothing but porter and skittles!'

Phipps Hornby was arguably the best naval officer of his day and he rose to be an Admiral of the Fleet, but, like many other naval officers of the time he remained sceptical of the new ironclads, or 'dummies', as he called them. When the squadron reached Yarmouth, he wrote to his wife 'We sail for Sunderland tomorrow, weather permitting. I have no idea how long we may be getting there. It is 190 miles—one day's sail for this ship; but if Sir F. Grey's dummies are to go under sail, I shall think it lucky if we get there in ten'.

In fact, it took five days, because the 'dummies' had to raise steam in their boilers ('tin pots', Phipps Hornby called them) to avoid some dangerous shoals off the Norfolk coast. When Phipps Hornby actually visited one of the ironclads (*Black Prince*) he thought her very fine, but criticised her vulnerable unarmoured ends and the fact that she had only three instead of four masts. The sailors in the ironclads, he found 'so disgustingly proud of their ships that they will allow them *no* faults'.

The general public shared this view and they flocked on board the ships in their thousands. The cruise was an astounding publicity success. As always, everybody wanted to see *Warrior*. At Sunderland, she had 24,285 visitors on board. Anchored in Leith roads, off Edinburgh, the ship was 'filled with visitors'. It was the same at anchor off Moville in Loch Foyle—'filled with visitors' from Londonderry. At Greenock, on 1 September, the ship was 'very full of visitors' from Glasgow and so it was at Carrickfergus, in Belfast Lough, open to visitors from Belfast. Everywhere the ships went, people gave balls and dinners, and organised festivities in the Navy's honour.

The climax of the cruise was the visit to Liverpool. The Squadron arrived in the Mersey, under sail, and anchored off Liverpool on 14 September. The ships were open to visitors for eight of the ten days until 24th. Once again, people swarmed on board in their thousands. Everybody was impressed by the great guns and exclaimed at the engines and the boats and the massive anchors, and commented on *Black Prince*'s 'telescopic funnels' and *Resistance*'s electric telegraph and her below decks gas lighting, similar to *Warrior*'s. In *Warrior*, the ladies particularly admired the laundry drying room (actually the brain-child of Captain Cochrane himself) fitted with a heating apparatus for drying the sailors' clothes in bad weather.

On 22 September, some hospitable gentlemen of Liverpool, members of the Royal Mersey Yacht Club, gave a special dinner for 800 bluejackets and 200 marines of the Channel Squadron at St George's Hall. The men, who had been specially chosen for their good behaviour, having never broken their leave in their present ships, landed at Prince's stage at noon in a gale of wind and rain. They were all well soaked by the time they moved off at 12.30.

Warrior **(right) with the Channel Squadron entering the Mersey in September 1863.**

However, nothing could dampen such an occasion. Preceded by a contingent of the Liverpool police and *Edgar*'s band, the men marched off by ship's companies. The *Warriors*, commanded by Lieutenant Fisher, marched behind a blue banner embroidered with the ship's crest, each man with a bouquet of flowers pinned to his breast.

The sailors were cheered all the way from the pierhead to the city centre, with special cheers for HMS *Liverpool*'s contingent. Huge crowds packed the sides of the route, hats were thrown into the air, every corner was decorated with flags, every window packed with waving, cheering watchers, the bells of St Nicholas pealed out, the cheers were deafening, the bands played and the police had to clear a way through. The sailors appeared amazed by this reception. One was quoted as saying, 'Well, we'll think ourselves somebodies after all this. Blow me if ever I see'd such a sight as this. Just let 'em attack Liverpool and send for the Channel Fleet, that's all.' They gave three cheers at Nelson's Monument and another three for the Queen, and arrived at St George's Hall shortly before two o'clock.

The Hall, too, was specially decorated with plants, flags, banners, the Royal Arms and a scroll: 'The Brave British Tars of Old England'. The men sat down at some 16 or 17 tables, by ship's companies, each table seating some 60 men. Every man had a small bottle of three-water grog and a quart bottle of Alsopp's Pale Ale.

The bill of fare was: 'Dinner—Beef, roast and boiled, Ham, baked and boiled Potatoes, and other vegetables; Remove—Plum pudding and Crimean sauce; Dessert— Apples, Ale and Punch'. When the guests had done justice to this, there were toasts, speeches, cheers,

recitations, songs and more cheers, the bluejackets and their hosts taking it in turns to perform, followed by more toasts and even more cheers, more beer, more songs and prolonged cheering.

According to Fisher, after the banquet was over, *Warrior*'s Captain of the Maintop, John Kiernan, climbed up on to his chair and, quite unsolicited, said: 'On behalf of his top-mates he wished to thank the Mayor and Corporation for a jolly good dinner and the best beer he'd ever tasted'. He stopped there and said: 'Bill, hand me up that beer again'. Bill said there was no more! A pledge had been given by the Mayor that they should have only two bottles of beer each. But this episode was too much for the Mayor, and instantly in came beer by the dozen, and my beloved friend, the Captain of the Maintop, had another glass. He said: 'This is joy' and he looked round the galleries crowded with the lovely ladies, and said 'Here we are, British Sailors entirely surrounded by females!!' They waved their hankerchiefs and kissed their hands, and that urged the Captain of the Maintop into a fresh flight of eloquence. 'Now,' he said, 'Shipmates, what was it like now coming into this 'ere harbour of Liverpool' (we had come in under sail); 'why', he said, 'this is what it was like, sailing into a haven of joy before a gale of pleasure.' I then told him to shut up, because he would spoil it by anything more . . .'

By the time they had toasted 'Sweethearts and Wives' and sung 'God Save the Queen', it was half past five o'clock. By then, some 60,000 people were lining the route back to the pier, waiting to give the sailors one last rousing send-off. Some women had placed themselves across the road and caused the bluejackets to break ranks. Matters then appeared to get out of hand, with sailors dancing through the streets, commandeering hansom cabs, riding on top and taking over the reins. When the *Warriors* looked as if they might be about to join the general jollifications, the quick-witted Fisher appealed to their 'honour and affection', thinking, as he said, 'they might have had a good lot of beer'. When they marched back to the boats in fours, Fisher asked them 'to take each other's arms. They nobly did it! And I got highly complimented for the magnificent way they marched back through the streets!'.

After a visit to Dublin, when again *Warrior* was 'filled with visitors', the Channel Squadron anchored in Plymouth Sound on 3 October, at the end of their twelve-week flag-showing cruise. The cruise had been a resounding success. The squadron had made twelve ports of call (eleven were official visits and one, to Inganess Bay in the Orkneys, was to take shelter from gales). *Warrior* herself had some staggering statistics. She had been visited by some 270,000 people, with visitors from yachts and small vessels estimated at another 30,000. The most visitors she had on one day was 14,273, at Sunderland. The greatest number of steamers she had had alongside her in one day was 194. Taking *Warrior*'s figures as an indication, it seems probable that over 1,600,000 people visited the Fleet during the cruise.

In April 1864, when *Warrior* was at Portland, Guiseppe Garibaldi came on board the ship during a visit to Weymouth. He witnessed the guns' crews at drill when, as Fisher wrote in a letter to his Aunt Kate '. . . we went to general quarters and commenced firing away like fun and went through all sorts of different evolutions with the guns; first we supposed the enemy on one bow and then on the other; in fact, the enemy was everywhere in the course of ten minutes. The men worked the guns splendidly. I never saw them move quicker before. Garibaldi turned round to me and said ''he was vary moch pleased indeed'', and he afterwards said it was almost the finest thing he had seen in England.' Garibaldi told the ship's company 'that he had seen one of the things he had set his heart on seeing, and that was the *Warrior*.'

Warrior's cruises in the rest of 1863 and in 1864 were to Madeira and to Teneriffe, to Lisbon again and to Gibraltar, to Bantry Bay and to Queenstown and several times to Portsmouth, Plymouth and Portland. On 1 November 1864, she anchored at Spithead and next day went into Portsmouth harbour, where she was lashed alongside the dockyard. For the next 2½ weeks, she prepared to pay off, de-ammunitioning, returning stores and gear (including the hydraulic steering gear which trials during the flag-showing cruise had shown to be a failure). On 22 November 1864, *Warrior* was paid off into the 2nd Division of the Reserve. Her log for that day recorded 'Sunset hauled down Pennant'.

2

Life in the Victorian Navy

'The Black Brigade' showing various punishments: For spitting on deck—carrying a spittoon around; for dirty clothing—carrying the clean article lashed to an oar; for slack hammock—carrying the properly lashed hammock over the shoulder. From the Boy's Own Paper, December 1890.

One of the guests who came on board *Warrior* during her visit to Liverpool in September 1863 afterwards wrote an account of what he saw and heard which, even today, still gives the reader a vivid 'sense of place', a sensation of actually walking along *Warrior*'s decks on a forenoon in the 1860s, while the ship's company were going about their normal life and duties.

'On visiting this celebrated ship—the ''Warrior'', yesterday, on stepping on to the upper deck, the scene was very imposing. The sun was reflected from the bright white deck of the ship, but the absence of fires on board, except for cooking purposes, rendered the position pleasant and agreeable. The rain of the previous night made it necessary to loose the sails to dry, which caused a constant noise of the flapping of the canvas to be kept up over head. Between the masts were hung in lines, fore and aft, the newly washed clothes of the men, which were not long in being thoroughly dried; there is also, below, a drying room for this purpose in bad weather, fitted with a heating apparatus. A lady remarked to her husband that she was more delighted with this washing feature than anything else she had seen on board; and added, that men-of-war's men must be clever handy fellows to be able thus to do their own washing.

Visitors are received on board with the greatest courtesy, and every one on board vies with each other to give more information. Several officers were going about with ladies and gentlemen, explaining the working of the Armstrong guns; and it was amusing to see the interest taken by the ladies in a subject which might be supposed to be rather unpleasant than otherwise. Along the broad white deck, which looked like a great broad street, men were seen rope making, carpentering, making hammocks, and hand ropes &c. Sentries were walking their quiet rounds as silently as if there were no crowd around them. Going down the ladder to the main deck, the ear was greeted with the bleeting of sheep, and the cackle of domestic fowls in spacious coops, and the animals seemed quite at home among plenty of clean fodder and food. Large quantities of butchers' meat hanging up ready for cooking. Cooks busy at work in the galley, preparing all sorts of dishes—the smell set up is savoury, and calculated to give one an appetite.

It is not yet meat time, yet here and there are seen some of the fine fellows leisurely (it being their watch below, as it is termed) dispatching their ''levener'', from the hour ''eleven'' at which it is taken; and which, in one instance, was a goodly snack of fried beefsteaks and onions; and another mutton chops and boiled rice; and in both cases plenty of biscuits. While a great many were eating, many were engaged in reading (Newspapers mostly) or writing letters; some working hearthrugs by a quilting process, or embroidering pictures. Many lay asleep, having to go on deck at twelve o'clock; some sat wrapt in their own meditation, as if unconscious of what was going on around them; one man, a marine, chaunted a song, with a fine cultivated voice; and an artillery-man tried to get up a laugh in his own mess, by pretending to read from a newspaper of a man being drowned by a cart wheel passing over him, but the joke was too stale.

It is generally understood on shore that ''Jack'', when not on duty, is passing round the grog or smoking, but here you found the seamen better occupied in their leisure moments: here was to be seen the quiet family man, who is melted into ''softness'' by the visit of his dearest female friend, and sits beside her apparently recalling many happy moments, or mending his clothes, or shoes, or doing the barber. We are all familiar with the British seaman as a daring man, and a light-hearted cheery man; we read of him as a hero, and we find him on shore with a soul lifted above all mean and common cares; but we have to visit him in his abode, in order to see him as the homely man.'

The same visitor observed two 68-pounder (sic) rifled Armstrong guns on the upper deck, and 'gun carriages for two field pieces, intended for a landing at any hostile place'. The upper deck had guns forward and aft but it was primarily a working deck, most of it left clear, open to the sky, where the ship was navigated and (usually) steered, where yards, sails and running rigging were handled, where boats and some of the anchors were lowered and hoisted, and where drills and evolutions were carried out.

The upper deck itself was of iron plate, but covered with broad planks 4″ thick and 8″ wide, which made a tremendous sweep of timber, scrubbed and holystoned until it gleamed white. It was enclosed by seven foot bulwarks, which ran right round the ship and almost completely obscured any view from the upper deck. This was a relic from the days of sail when such bulwarks were needed to protect the men working the upper deck guns; no such protection was needed in *Warrior* but the bulwarks were still fitted. Along the tops of the bulwarks were hammock racks covered with canvas toppings where the ship's company's hammocks were stowed when not in use.

A Sailor in Naval Uniform of 1860.

As the Liverpool visitor remarked, the best view of the upper deck was from one or other of the light navigating bridges which stretched across almost the whole width of the deck. The forward bridge was just aft of the forward funnel, which was telescopic and could be retracted when the ship was under sail; the funnels were painted black when the ship first commissioned, but a pale buff colour from late 1863 onwards, and in all her later commissions.

Looking forward, the visitor would see the great soaring bowsprit with its associated rigging, the bow chaser guns, the forward hatchways and the foremast with its shrouds and ratlines outboard, and the bitts (for securing sail halliards) at its foot.

Above, rising so high the visitor would have to crane his head back, was the great dramatic pattern of masts, yards, crosstrees and standing rigging. The yards, like the funnels, were black on commissioning but light yellow after about July 1867. *Warrior* was rigged, the official specification stated, 'as for a 80-gun ship of the line'. This meant she had three masts, Fore, Main and Mizzen. The distance from fore and main trucks (the tops of the masts) to the deck was 175 feet. The fore and main yards (the largest) were 105 feet long. The total sail area, not including stunsails, was about 33,400 square feet. The fore or main topsail in *Warrior* was about 4,000 square feet, with leeches of about 60 feet and 95 feet from clew to clew. This was about the largest sail that thirty men (the most that could get on the yard at one time) could humanly handle in a gale.

Immediately abreast of the bridge, if one looked down on the ship's side port and starboard, were the sailors' heads (with more up forward, on either side of the bowsprit rigging, but these were often unusable in rough weather).

Aft from the bridge were more hatchways, the after funnel (also telescopic) with the ventilators alongside it, and some of the ship's boats. The number and type of boats did vary but normally *Warrior* had two 42 foot launches, stowed on the upper deck, amidships, one on each side. The starboard launch had a 20 foot gig stowed inside it, with a 14 foot dinghy stowed inside that; similarly, the port launch had a 32 foot pinnace stowed inside it.

Aft, there was a pair of davits on each side, with a 20 foot gig and a 30 foot cutter on the starboard side, and a 32 foot galley and another cutter on the port side. Right aft, on its own davits, hanging over the stern gallery, was an 18 foot jolly-boat. The ship's armament included three guns for the boats: one 25-pounder Armstrong and one 24-pounder howitzer for the launches, and a 12-pounder Armstrong for the pinnace.

Beyond the boats was the main mast, with its shrouds, ratlines and bitts. The best place to see the after end of the upper deck and its fittings was from a second bridge, also running the full width of the ship, just aft of the capstan. This was normally the navigating bridge, with the engine telegraphs and, a few feet aft, the four hand-worked main steering wheels.

Below the bridge, and immediately forward of it, was a rifle-proof conning tower, made of teak 12" thick, overlaid by iron plates 3" thick. It was about six foot high, with loopholes cut in the sides and an access ladder leading down to the upper deck. There was also a hole cut in the deck so that orders could be given to the helmsmen on the main deck below. Some old-fashioned officers, with Nelsonian ideas about personal bravery, deplored the con-

ning tower and complained that it spoiled the look of the ship. But if *Warrior* had ever had to lie close alongside an enemy, as she was designed to do, the officers on her deck would have been very vulnerable to small arms fire and the conning tower was intended to give them some protection.

The ship was normally steered from the steering position just aft of the conning tower where there were the main compass and the steering compasses, but in action, or in rough weather the ship could be steered from the main deck. The screw well, in which the propellor was hoisted and lowered, was immediately in front of the rudder-post, so it was not possible to have a single straight tiller as in many sailing ships. Instead, a yoke was fitted with crosshead arms long enough to extend beyond the screw well on either side. The yoke arms were connected to the steering wheels by ropes made of leather thongs, led forward through a series of tackles and sheaves.

Each steering position had four wheels, six feet in diameter. From hard a port to hard a starboard took 3½ turns of the wheel. It was intended that the ship should normally be steered by four quartermasters, but *Warrior*'s designers had not realised that screw propulsion involved special problems of steering. Throughout her life *Warrior* was a brute to steer. Sometimes there were as many as sixteen men hauling on the spokes with, occasionally, even more men in the tiller flat below hauling on relieving tackles on the yoke crosshead.

Further aft was the mizzen mast, the ladder hatchway leading down to the officers' cabins, the skylight for the Captain's cabin, and the 100-pounder stern pivot gun with its elegantly curved metal runners set into the deck allowing it to be slewed from side to side to fire through a choice of seven gun ports.

Right aft was the ensign staff, which flew the White Ensign on *Warrior*'s commissioning but was soon flying the Red. Until 5 August 1864, when the system was changed by Admiralty order, all flag officers except Admirals of the Fleet were divided by seniority in their ranks into three imaginary 'Squadrons'—the Blue, the White and the Red in ascending order of seniority—and ships flew the ensign appropriate to their flag officers' seniority. Thus, when Rear Admiral Robert Smart, Rear Admiral of the White, was on board in 1862, *Warrior* flew the White Ensign. But in 1863, when Smart was promoted to the Red, the Red Ensign was flown. Similarly, in 1863, Rear Admiral Sydney Dacres flew his flag in *Warrior* as Rear Admiral of the White, with the White Ensign, and in 1864 as Rear Admiral of the Red, with the Red Ensign. *Warrior* therefore flew the Red Ensign from the second quarter of 1862 until 23 April 1863, and again from the fourth quarter of 1863 until August 1864. Thenceforth, like every commissioned ship in the Navy, she wore the White Ensign.

To a visitor, the overwhelming impression of *Warrior*'s upper deck is one of enormous emptiness, of seemingly acres of space compared with a modern ship's upper deck. The space was needed. Every major evolution was done

Night Alarm—prepared for action c1870.

by hand and there had to be room for the sheer numbers of men who provided the muscle power.

Some prodigious weights were involved. The fore and main yards weighed six tons. The bronze two-bladed Griffith's propellor, 23½ feet in diameter and the largest hoisting screw ever made (except for that in *Black Prince*) was often disconnected from the shaft and hauled up for long passages under sail. It weighed 10 tons, while the 'banjo frame' which hoisted the propellor was itself 7 tons. Even the sheer legs rigged for this evolution weighed four tons. Thus, 'hoisting the ruddy old twiddler' required lower deck to be cleared of both watches, each watch manning the falls on its own side, 600 men on the falls.

Warrior had four Admiralty pattern 5½ ton wooden-stocked anchors—two bower anchors forward and two sheet anchors stowed outboard in the fore part of the waist, with hinged iron crutches to throw them clear of the ship's side when let go. She also had two 2½ ton Rodgers-type stern anchors, one iron-stocked stream anchor weighing a ton and a half, and two iron-stocked kedge anchors, each just under a ton. The anchors were weighed by hand, using a method dating from medieval times.

The anchor cables were chain, and not hemp hawsers as in the days of sail, but the cables were still led in the old way, not directly to the capstan, but along the main deck to the cable lockers abreast the main mast by means of a 'messenger'. The old massive hemp cables had been too thick to wrap around the barrel of the capstan. Instead, three turns of a much smaller cable or 'messenger' was taken around the capstan, on the main deck aft. The messenger was then led forward, guided by means of rollers set in the main deck to a manger in the bows whence it returned down the other side of the ship, back to the capstan.

The messenger thus formed an endless chain, worked by the capstan, moving forward up one side of the ship and aft down the other, or in the reverse direction, depending upon which anchor, port or starboard, was being hoisted. As the anchor cable itself came up through the hawsepipe, it was stopped to the messenger by 'nippers'— small lengths of rope—which were wound on and unwound by sailors specially chosen for their skill, alertness and agility. Two of these smart hands would face each other, up forward where the cable came in through the hawsepipe, and between them wind on the nippers fastening the cable to the messenger. The cable was then hauled aft along the main deck, with the messenger actually taking the strain of hoisting. Aft were two more smart hands, unwinding the nippers and disengaging the cable from the messenger just before the cable disappeared down into the chain locker.

The capstan had two barrels, of which the upper, actually on the upper deck, was normally manned. With eighteen capstan bars, five men to each bar, and another twenty men on the 'swifter' (the rope running between the ends of the capstan bars), the capstan had room for more than a hundred men who, when hoisting, looked like 'a densely packed human whirlpool', reeling round

ILLUSTRATED LONDON NEWS 25 JAN 1862

Carving the meat for dinner—and serving out the grog.

and round, and stamping in time to the music of the ship's band.

All *Warrior's* people were subject to a rigid hierarchical structure of command which, broadly, has survived into the Navy of today. The Captain, the Hon. Arthur Cochrane, was king. He was responsible to the Admiralty for everybody and everything on board. If matters went well, it was to the Captain's credit. If badly, the Captain was to blame. The mid-Victorian Captain did not have quite the absolute powers of Captains in the days of sail, but he was still as near to the deity as made no practical difference to those beneath him, especially in a detached ship on a foreign station in an era before the coming of wireless. He could if he wished, 'assume the god, affect to nod'.

Such power left its mark on a man. The Sultan of Morocco, visiting a British battleship of the 1880s, was asked what had impressed him most—the guns, the engines, the torpedo boats, the electric light? 'The Captain's face' was his reply. The Admiralty, always sensitive to public criticism about naval punishments, could and did reprimand and even relieve a brutal and tyrannical captain. But, given such power over others, the wonder is not that the occasional captain was corrupted by it but that so many, like Cochrane, were very highly re-

garded and respected by their ship's companies.

As befitted his position on board, the Captain had spacious quarters aft on the main deck, with a large day cabin for dining and entertaining, and separate sleeping cabin. There was a Captain's pantry, forward in the next flat, and a Captain's office. The Captain also had his own heads, on the starboard side aft. In *Warrior* the Captain's quarters were not in the traditional aftermost part, or gallery. This was largely occupied by the rudder yoke crosshead and the screw-well. Thus the 'gallery windows' painted on the outside were fakes.

On the starboard side of the main deck, forward of the Captain, Commander George Tryon had his cabin. The Commander was the ship's second-in-command and the Captain's right-hand man. He would take charge of the ship in the Captain's death or absence. He was responsible to the Captain for the ship's fighting ability, smartness and cleanliness. He was also *ex officio* president of the wardroom mess.

The only other officer to have his cabin on the main deck, on the opposite port side to the Commander, was the Master, George H. Blakey—although he, like the Commander, had to share his cabin with a 68-pounder gun and the wooden partitions of all these cabins, even the Captain's, could be removed at action stations.

The Master was a member of a branch which is no longer present in the modern Navy. He ranked with the Lieutenants, but after them. He would not take command of the ship so long as any of the Lieutenants survived. He was the ship's navigating officer and was the Captain's expert on the subject (although the Captain remained ultimately responsible for the ship's safety at sea). The Master took sun and star sights. He kept the deck log. He was responsible for the rigging and stores with the Boatswain as his immediate junior. He conned the ship in action. He was likely to be one of the ship's 'old and bold', something of a 'character', with a flavour of the 'old Navy' about him; he would tend to be older than the rest of the wardroom and would often have come up from the lower deck—the only member of the mid-Victorian wardroom who could do so.

Warrior had five lieutenants and watch-keepers: in order of seniority, Henry B. Phillimore (who became an admiral), first and gunnery lieutenant; Joseph E. Wilson; George F. H. Parker; Henry L. Perceval; and Noel S. F. Digby. The lieutenants, normally aged between twenty-five and thirty-five, must have served at least six years at sea and theirs was the highest rank which could be achieved without selection; some lieutenants remained in the rank for many years. The lieutenants took charge of a watch on deck and would command one of the larger boats in a boat expedition. They were also given charge of one of the 'tops', with special responsibility for the sailors in that top.

Other members of the wardroom were three officers of the marine artillery, soon to become the Royal Marine Artillery: Captain Henry W. Mawbey; Lieutenant Herbert Everitt; and 2nd Lt Francis H. E. Owen. The Paymaster, who was responsible for pay, clothing, victualling and accounts on board, the ship's books, certificates, records of conduct, savings, allotments and remittances was John N. de Vries. The Revd Robert N. Jackson, was Chaplain and Naval Instructor, responsible for the school-work of the midshipmen. The Surgeon was Samuel S. D. Wells, who had two assistant surgeons, William J. Asslin and Edmund W. Coleman (Coleman's cabin was by the gunroom but he messed in the wardroom).

The wardroom officers had cabins on the lower deck. There were fourteen cabins, seven a side, measuring six feet by about ten, and spartanly furnished with a bunk, a collapsible table, a washstand with basin and jug, and personal additions such as a carpet, bookshelves, cushions, pictures and ornaments. Each cabin had a tiny round scuttle which admitted very little light. Candles and oil-lamps had to be used at all hours of the day, and all the year round.

The cabins had sliding doors opening on to a central wardroom mess with a large table (which, at action stations, was cleared for use as an operating table). Here the officers ate, relaxed and gossiped. They had to provide their own mess furniture, even the wardroom dining chairs, but most tried to make their mess more comfortable, with carpets, small tables, armchairs (if there was room), mirrors, a rack for newspapers and magazines, pictures on the bulkheads, sometimes potted plants, even a piano, and a formal portrait of Queen Victoria.

There was a large skylight in the deckhead and another above in the upper deck, so that the wardroom was comparatively well-lit and, on a fine day when conditions were right, might even get some sunlight—a great rarity in a Victorian man-of-war. Aft of the wardroom was a pantry, with a small galley and a crockery store used by the wardroom stewards. Aft of that again was the Captain's storeroom.

The junior officers—the sub-lieutenants (who used to be called Mates), the midshipmen and naval cadets, who would have been to the recently instituted officers' training ship HMS *Britannia*, the second-master and the master's assistants, the clerk and the clerk's assistants—lived in the Gunroom forward of the wardroom, often referred to as the 'steerage' (the old-fashioned 'cockpit'). On the starboard side in *Warrior* were an office and a pantry, and Coleman's cabin. Amidships was the main gunroom mess, with rows of drawer units and washbasins ranged around the bulkheads. It was lit from above by a skylight. On the port side was the dining room, with a table, lit by three tiny scuttles.

Here the young gentlemen, usually between 20 and 30 of them, led a jolly, somewhat troglodytic, communal existence, eating, washing, changing, studying, writing up their journals, ragging and sky-larking. They kept their belongings in sea chests stowed in a chest room aft; to reach it they had to climb up to the maindeck and down again through a ladder hatchway to a dark noisome compartment, lit by candles or lamps, where there were some 30 sea chests placed in rows amongst other various gear and impedimenta such as water tanks, hawsers and spare shot. The gunroom officers all slept in hammocks, not normally in the gunroom itself, but wherever they could find, with permission, hammock billets in nearby flats and passageways.

All midshipmen were (and still are) required to keep journals, in which they recorded with sketches and charts their own and the ship's doings. One of *Warrior*'s midshipmen, Henry Arthur Keith Murray, a fourteen-year-old who joined the ship in 1861, drew for his journal large detailed plans of the ship's decks, with everything marked in the place where it was stowed. The other midshipmen were puzzled by such industry; what was the point of it? Surely everybody knew where everything was—they saw it every day.

Although engineers had been given commissioned rank equal to the navigating masters in 1847, when their names had first appeared in the Navy List, only *Warrior*'s first and second Chief Engineers, William Buchan and William Glasspole (the Commander (E) and the Senior Engineer in a 20th Century warship) had wardroom cabins and status. The other ten engineers and assistant engineers had their own separate sleeping quarters and mess on the lower deck forward of the boiler rooms and above the forward magazine. Engineers were allowed to wear gold lace stripes on their sleeves in 1860 (although without the 'executive' curl) but were not admitted to the wardroom, unless they were Chief Engineers, until 1883.

Below the wardroom, officers were the senior warrant officers, the Boatswain, the Gunner and the Carpenter, who also had their own cabins forward on the lower deck next to the engineers' mess. Below them were the supernumary warrant officers, who were the mates of the various decks.

Then came the chief petty officers: the Master at Arms, who was head of the ship's police; the Chief Gunner's Mate, usually a gunnery instructor, who assisted the Gunnery Lieutenant in the gunnery instruction on board; the Chief Boatswain's Mate; the Chief Captain of the Forecastle, in charge of head booms and anchor gear; the Chief Signalman, later titled Chief Yeoman of Signals; the Chief Quartermaster, in charge of hand-wheels, tiller-ropes, and compasses, under the Master; the Chief Carpenters' Mate; the Seaman Schoolmaster, in charge, under the Chaplain, of the boys' education and men's voluntary studies; the Ship's Steward, in charge, under the Paymaster, of victualling and storage and the issue of clothing; and the Ship's Cook, in charge of the galley and general cooking for the ship's company. These chief petty officers would have their own mess, with a boy from each watch told off to clean the mess, fetch the food and generally act as 'messdeck dodger'.

Next were the first class petty officers, who were captains of the tops, the forecastle, main top, foretop and quarterdeck, and the gunner's mates. They supervised and were responsible for the work done by, and the conduct of, the men in their tops. The captains of the tops looked after all the gear above the top on their respective masts, the gunner's mates taking the main mast, and the captains of the forecastle taking the foreyards and lower rigging. First class petty officers were usually captains of guns and right-hand markers of the small arms companies for shore landing parties.

Also petty officers, first class, were the quartermasters, who kept regular watches on deck at sea, under the Lieutenants and the midshipmen, taking regular tricks on the steering wheel, acting as leadsmen in the chains, to take soundings when the ship was entering or leaving harbour, or going through a narrow passage, or approaching land; the boatswain's mates, who also kept watches and passed by pipe and voice all orders for turning up the hands, changing the watch or part of the watch, and assisting in seeing that ropes were manned and yards trimmed; and such individual ratings as the Captain's coxswain, the coxswain of the launch, the captain of the hold, the sailmaker, ropemaker, carpenter's mates, caulker, armourer, and the blacksmith. The second class petty officers assisted the first class, aloft and on deck, and were

Everyone turns to—Coaling Ship.

19

*Warrior's **officers on deck. A member of the boats crew made the photo too** . . .*

usually petty officers of the messes, one petty officer to a mess.

The aftermost messes on the main deck were occupied by the marine detachment. They were, as in 20th Century warships, placed nearest the officers' quarters and were called, then as today, the 'barracks'. The sergeant-major and the sergeants had a small mess to themselves. The marines provided guards and sentries around the ship, and took part in the sail drill and evolutions. Several of the main deck guns were crewed entirely by marines.

The rate of leading seaman, new when *Warrior* first commissioned, was instituted as part of the new career structure for the sailor. Leading seamen were chosen from the best and keenest of the able seamen and they had to pass a stiff examination in seamanship, and show that they merited being advanced in rate. They were then entitled to an extra 2d. a day. They were often put in charge of small working parties, after the pipe 'one hand from each part of ship to muster'. Entering harbour or approaching soundings, they were placed in the chains next to the quartermasters. The three best leading seamen in *Warrior* were made captains of the crosstrees, with responsibility for upper yard work.

Some 600 of the 700 men on board were required purely for their muscle power, although in the case of the guns' crews and the yardmen it was skilled muscle power. They were needed to hoist sails, haul on ropes, turn the capstans, hoist and lower boats, pull on oars, man the long-handled Downton pumps which provided water for firefighting and pumped out the bilges, and train and elevate the guns. Ruptures were an occupational disease of sailors in the ironclads, just as they had been in the days of sail.

These 600 men lived on the main deck which ran continuously from forward to aft, with only two divisions, the forward and after bulkheads of the armoured citadel. The two inboard passages on the main deck were the main thoroughfares of the ship along which, as the Liverpool visitor noted, sentries were passing on their rounds, seamen and stokers going on and off watch, and men carrying out ship's duties and errands of all kinds.

The four doors, one on each side, forward and aft, cut in the transverse bulkhead of the citadel show how thick the armour is. But the headroom on the main deck was several inches more than the sailors would have been used to in earlier ships and the messes were generally spacious and comfortable by the standards of the time.

The whole ship's company lived in 'broadside' messes, numbered (like the guns) odd numbers on the starboard side, even numbers to port, in the spaces between the guns on the main deck. There were 28 messes within the citadel, and six outside, which gives an average of about 18 men to a mess.

Each mess had a table which could be triced up to the deck head when scrubbing out the mess deck, or removed altogether at action stations or when coaling ship. Every mess also had two benches, a crockery rack on the outboard bulkhead with a basin, plate and spoon for every man, a rum tub, a bread barge and various utensils such as kettles and cans. A man was expected to use his own seaman's knife at table. Every utensil and item of crockery was clearly and indelibly marked with the number of the mess. Any losses had to be made good by the members. Above, in the deck beams, were hooks for hammocks, each set the regulation distance of 24½″ apart. Also secured to the deckhead above the mess were the rammers, sponges and worms used while loading and working the nearby guns.

Memories of messdeck life tend to be much more romantic than the reality. Living conditions on a mid-Victorian messdeck were vividly described by Admiral George Ballard, who joined the 'Black Fleet' battleship *Resistance* in the Channel Squadron in 1877: 'The bare bleakness of the mess-deck with its long range of plank tables and stools had as little suggestion of physical ease as a prison cell. It was damp and chilly in a cold climate, and damp and hot in the tropics. It was swept by searching draughts if the ports were open, and nearly pitch dark if they were closed, glass scuttles not having been invented. It was dimly lit at night by tallow candles inside lamps at long intervals, and as there were no drying rooms it reeked of wet serge and flannel in rainy weather. In short the living quarters of the mid-Victorian bluejacket, stoker, or marine were as widely dissociated from any ideal of a home in the usual sense as could well be imagined'.

'Moreover, he was always in a crowd by day or night. His work and his leisure, his eating, drinking, washing and sleeping were all in crowded surroundings. He swallowed his bully beef and hard tack, his pea soup, 'copper rattle', and rum, at a mess table so congested that he had absolutely no elbow room and scarce space to sit. He washed himself twice a week on deck at the same time as he washed his clothes, in the two tubfuls of cold water which formed the allowance for the whole twenty-five men in his mess, in the middle of a splashing mob at other tubs all round; and he slung his hammock at night among hundreds of others so tightly packed that they had no swinging room however much the ship rolled. Even in the head he had no individual privacy'.

So that a large number of men could live, work, sleep, eat, keep their kit and belongings and entertain themselves in such very confined limits, every man had an allotted space on board, and naval discipline demanded (and ensured) that he stay in his place. Every man had an allotted 'quarter', for action stations or for a fire alarm. Every man (except the idlers, such as cooks, stewards, stores assistants) was either in the port or starboard watch for duty. He also had a 'part of ship', forecastle, foretop, maintop or quarterdeck, for work aloft. He would have a ship's book number, for payment and for muster by open list. He had his allotted rack on the lower deck for his bag (ditty boxes could normally be stowed in the mess) and his own billet for his hammock.

For example, a particular able seaman would be number 457 in the ship's book, in the starboard watch, a foretop-man, and Number Three (loader) on No. 4 gun on the main deck. He was a member of No. 28 Mess, took an oar in the starboard pinnace, and slept in hammock number 240, which he stowed in the larboard (i.e. port) waist hammock nettings.

In *Warrior*, the main deck gunports had bullet-proof iron lids, raised and lowered by tackles from inside the ship. Each lid had a small viewing port cut in its centre. The ship's company preferred the port lids, and indeed all the hatches leading to the upper deck, to be kept firmly shut at all times. The sailors were not concerned with ventilation or hygiene. They wanted a 'fug', the thicker the better. They got all the fresh air they wanted, and more, doing drills on the upper deck.

The citadel was one compartment but it was effectively divided into two, port and starboard, with cross-passages at intervals, by a range of equipment and compartmentation amidships such as the funnel casings, the galley, the capstans, pens and coops for livestock, water tanks, the main deck steering position, and the several hatches leading down to the lower deck.

Below was the lower deck and what were known as 'the flats'—a miscellany of compartments including store rooms and issue rooms, magazine handling rooms, some cabins, bag racks, sail bins, the dispensary, sail room, the cells, and bathrooms.

Below again was the orlop deck, on which were the engine room and boiler rooms, the magazines and, aft, the propellor shaft tunnel.

Warrior's stokers and trimmers had physically the hardest job of any on board. The ship had eight coal bunkers, placed alongside and outboard of the engine room and boiler rooms, containing 850 tons of coal—every ounce of which had to be shovelled by hand, first from the back to the front of the bunkers and then from the bunkers to the furnace doors and there flung in, sometimes for a distance of several feet, to wherever the fiery layer of coal was beginning to look thin.

The side bunkers placed behind the boilers on each side of the ship were nearly 100 feet long. To save labour, the ship had its own G.W.R.—the Great *Warrior* Railway, with small coal trucks running on rails. The trucks were emptied by another labour-saving device—a side flap which was lifted to let the coal run out on to the deck. Even harder physical work than firing the boilers was breaking up and removing the quantities of ash and the huge lumps of clinker left behind. The boiler footplate temperature was usually around 90°F. During the record-breaking speed run in October 1861, it rose to 129°F.

The coal had also to be brought on board and stowed in the bunkers by hand. *Warrior* spent a reasonable amount of time under sail, and for her ship's company coaling was not the frequent and exhausting ordeal it became later in the 19th Century and in the early part of the 20th Century. Nevertheless, coaling ship was done as an evolution in which all hands took part. In time ships in company came to treat it as a contest, ship against ship, squadron against squadron, and competed to achieve the fastest rate of coaling per hour and the shortest total coaling time, indicating with flag hoists their rate of progress.

The sacks of coal were hauled up out of the hold of the collier alongside and manhandled inboard through the gunports, while the ship's band would play encouraging tunes on the upper deck. The sacks were pulled on trolleys along the main deck to shutes to be emptied into the bunkers below, where men stood ready with shovels to trim the coal evenly. The main deck was, of course, the ship's company's living quarters and though the guns were covered in canvas to save them from the dust, and all mess deck tables and fittings would be removed beforehand, it was not long before the whole main deck was as black with coal dust as the men themselves. Always, after coaling, the hands had to spend a considerable time scrubbing, washing down and cleaning their messdecks to make them habitable once again. The only compensations the men had while coaling ship were that they could wear what clothes they liked and they could smoke as they liked.

The older members of Warrior's ship's company would have entered the Navy under the old casual scheme, when a man served for a ship's commission and was discharged at the end of it, to re-engage or not, as he liked. But, just as Warrior herself was a ship from a new era, so most of her

sailors were the products of a new scheme of naval entry and training. From 1 July 1853, all new boy entrants to the Navy engaged for ten years' continuous service, their 'man's time' to start from the age of eighteen. Boys and seamen already serving were encouraged to transfer from the old system, although the sailor's freedom to choose his ships remained under both schemes. Under the new scheme, after ten years' service a sailor could re-engage for a further ten years to complete his time for pension.

Most of Warrior's sailors would have entered as boys through the old 'Guardho' training ship Illustrious at Portsmouth. There, in a six month course, they were taught elementary knots and hitches, and how to lash up a hammock; boat pulling and how to dip, toss and feather oars; cutlass and rifle drill, how to march and present arms, and how to aim and fire; how to exercise on the big guns, how to load, fire and dismount a gun, and how to use the various items of equipment to serve the guns; how to splice and do more complicated knots, such as the 'Matthew Walker' and 'Turk's Head'; learn the names and uses of all the ropes and sails in a ship; how to use the lead-line, box the compass, and steer a ship to a given course. They would also go to sea for three months in the training brig Sealark to learn sail drill, and how to work aloft.

In short, the Illustrious boys had a first-class grounding

The Armstrong Upper Deck Gun, Photographed in 1861.

in the elements of their profession and they came to sea, certainly as raw newcomers, but as trained hands nonetheless. Seamen-gunners would also have passed a course in gunnery at *Excellent*, in which they (and their officers) would have had instruction in the particular types of guns fitted in their ships. A qualified seaman gunner received an extra 4d. a day, in the first class, and 2d. a day in the second class. They were also allowed to count five years' service as six for pension.

The new boy entrant to *Illustrious*, the 'nozzer' as he was called, was given a standard issue of uniform clothing: one pair of blue cloth trousers, two blue serge frocks (a frock had full length loose sleeves, buttoned at the wrist-band with two buttons, and unlike the jumper was tucked inside the waistband of the trousers), two pairs of white duck trousers, two white jumpers, two pairs of stockings, two white frocks, three flannels, two caps, a seaman's knife, and a type for marking his name. This, with a bed and blanket, cost £3 10s.

In 1857 the sailor's uniform was at last definitely laid down by regulation, and became more or less standardised—there was still room for personal idiosyncracies in dress about which an exasperated Admiralty was complaining until the end of the 19th century. The uniform consisted of a blue serge frock, with a jumper added later as an alternative; blue collar bordered with white tape; blue cloth jacket or 'tunic', which was like an officer's mess jacket, with black buttons; blue cloth trousers; duck or white drill frock and white duck trousers, as alternatives to the serge and cloth; pea jacket; black silk handkerchief; sennet straw hat, black or white according to the climate; blue cloth cap; badges of rank for Petty officers. There were no uniform shirts. They varied, being white, blue, coloured or check, made of flannel or cloth. Boots were issued but were worn as little as possible. The soles of sailors' feet became flattened by the decks and as hard as leather, so that many sailors were acutely uncomfortable in boots or shoes.

There were also small rises in sailors' pay in the 1860s so that a chief petty officer earned 2s. 3d. a day or £41 1s. 3d. (41.06½p) a year. Similarly, a first class petty officer's pay was 2s. (10p) a day; a second class petty officer, 1s. 10d.; a leading seaman, 1s. 9d.; an able seaman, 1s. 7d.; an ordinary seaman, 1s. 3d.; a second class ordinary seaman, 1s.; a boy first class or a naval apprentice, 7d. a day; and a second class boy 6d. a day or £9 2s. 6d. (£9.12½p) a year.

As would be expected, officers' pay was higher. Captain Cochrane was paid £1 a day, Commander Tryon 16s. 6d., Master George Blakey, 13s. 6d., a senior Lieutenant, 11s. a day, a junior, 10s. The highest paid officer on board *Warrior* was the Paymaster, at 26s. a day, the lowest a Naval Cadet at 11d. a day.

The changes in the system of entry and training constituted a major reform in what was then, as always, a fiercely conservative Royal Navy. But, as the pattern of his daily life and routine shows, the Victorian sailor was still subject to the Navy's traditionally draconian code of discipline.

3

A Day on board *Warrior*

Make and mend clothes . . .

A warship in commission, like a great country house, never slept. Whatever the hour of day or night, there was always somebody awake, on watch or on rounds. The daily shipboard routine followed a broadly similar pattern throughout the year, although there were some variations in the times laid down for routines in harbour and at sea, and for summer and winter. The day's progress was marked out by the ship's bell, struck every half hour, and the shrilling of the boatswain's calls. A ship's bell was not tolled, like a church bell, but struck briskly, e.g. 'bong-bong . . . bong-bong' for four bells.

In *Warrior*, as in every ship, the sailors' day always be-

gan very early, at sea with 'coil up ropes' at 3.30am, followed by 'scrub decks' at 4am. After the decks had been scrubbed, the sails re-set and awnings spread, hammocks were lashed up and stowed at 6.15. At 6.30 a bugle sounded for cooks of the messes to go to the galley. All hands went to breakfast at 6.45.

In harbour, the boatswain's mates, ship's corporals and mates of decks were called at 4.40am in summer (5.10 in winter). Hands were called five minutes later, by the boatswain's mates running to and fro along the main deck blowing shrill notes on their boatswain's calls and roaring 'Rouse out here!—rouse out! show a leg!'

The men fell in to scrub the upper and half deck at 4.50, while duty boats' crews cleaned out their boats. The decks were first soaked with water, then holy-stoned with hand stones until they were covered with a thin grey paste. More water was poured on, and the paste rubbed and swept away with brooms until the wood of the deck reappeared 'white as a barked tree'. The deck was then wiped dry and 'dumb-scraped'.

'Lash up and stow' was at 6am, 'cooks to the galley' at 6.15. For breakfast, at half past six, the men had bowls of hot cocoa, heated in a huge copper in the galley, in which they dipped their ship's biscuit.

The hands had half an hour for breakfast, so at 7am in harbour (7.15 at sea) the watch coming on deck (the Forenoon) mustered in working rig. The duty quarter-masters, signalmen and duty boats' crews wore the rig of the day. The different rigs for different work in a Victorian battleship were not rigidly laid down by regulation, but the usual custom was for duty men and duty boats' crews to wear blue serge jumpers, check shirts and blue cloth trousers in cold or temperate climates, and white duck jumpers with white trousers in the tropics. On Mondays, Fridays and Saturdays the rest of the hands wore white working dress—over blue in cold weather. On Tuesdays, Wednesdays and Thursdays everyone wore the same as the duty men. After evening quarters and drills, at sea and in harbour, hands were piped to shift into 'night clothing'—normally a shirt, blue trousers and in cold weather a jumper.

On Monday afternoons, for general drills, and on Friday forenoons, for battle drills, everyone wore white working dress until the drills were over, when the duty men and duty boats crews were piped to shift into blue clothing. On Sundays everybody wore blue serge frocks, check shirts, and blue cloth trousers. But sometimes Sunday rig was a white cotton frock, with blue jean collar and wristbands, worn under a blue cloth 'tunic'. Hats were always worn on Sundays except in wet weather—black glazed hat in winter, white sennet hat in summer.

After mustering, when the roll was called by the Midshipman of the watch, the Forenoon watchmen cleaned bright work, while the upper yardmen cleaned the lightning conductors on the masts. Meanwhile the watch below scrubbed and cleaned the main and lower decks and flats. Decks were constantly being wetted, washed down and scrubbed in Victorian men-of-war, just as they had been in the days of sail. Thus, the decks below were almost always damp and tuberculosis was a serious health risk amongst sailors.

At 7.30 the forenoon watch fell in again for the morning evolution—normally replacing the gear aloft sent down the night before: on Monday and Tuesday, royal yards, on Wednesday and Thursday cross upper yards from top-gallants down, and on Friday cross royal yards, then prepare for action aloft by sending down top-gallant masts and all booms, bracing up yards, running head booms and toggling braces.

After the morning evolution, at 8am it was 'Hands to quarters, clean guns', and the hands were piped to clean, after which rifles, cutlasses and pistols were cleaned. Pump gear was cleaned on Mondays and Wednesdays. On Tuesdays and Thursdays the bugle sounded for the men to put on webbing belts, and men bearing small arms fell in by companies and were inspected by their lieutenants. One morning a week, landing parties were exercised, with small arms men, field guns, pioneers, stretcher bearers and the ship's band.

After drills, the drum roll cleared all hands off the lower deck. The Commander and the First Lieutenant went on rounds. 'Ready for morning quarters' was reported to the Captain and the bugle sounded again for men to fall in by divisions. The men were inspected and reported correct by their Lieutenants. Prayers were read on the quarterdeck, or on the main deck in rainy weather.

The hands then worked in their parts of ship during the forenoons. At 9.45 there would be a drill for the watch on deck, usually shifting a spar or a sail. At 10am there were regular drills for the instruction of untrained men. One of the quarters i.e. a proportion of the guns' crews, would be exercised under the Gunnery Lieutenant. The ordinary seaman and boys were instructed in seamanship—knots and splices, or going aloft, loosing, furling and reefing sails, sending down royal yards under the First Lieutenant and instructors.

On Monday forenoons, there were general exercises and drills aloft. On Wednesdays, an anchor and cable gear would be laid out. On another day, the ship's boats would be manned and armed. The mid-Victorian Royal Navy had not had a fleet or even a ship to ship engagement for years, but it was seldom that a ship's commission went by without her having to land armed parties, or even a full-scale Naval Brigade, to put down an insurrection or put out a fire.

When other ships were in company, evolutions were always carried out with fierce competitiveness. In a peacetime Navy, promotion often depended upon drills. The signal from the admiral 'Evolution well executed' would send morale soaring on board the ship named. Similarly, 'Repeat the evolution' spread gloom on deck for days.

All sail drill, and indeed almost every part of every evolution or drill, was carried out in strict silence. The loudest noise was the padding of the men's bare feet as they went about the decks. At the order 'Still', every man froze just where he was, no matter how awkward or grotesque his stance at the time.

In their understandable anxiety to beat other ships, the sailors often took undue risks and there were many falls from aloft. Admiral Ballard recalled that when he was a midshipman in *Achilles* in 1877/78 there were twelve fatal falls from the rigging in one Mediterranean commission. Ballard said he remembered all his life 'the sickening horror with which as quite a youngster I first saw a blue-clad human figure whirling down with an awful rush from a hundred and fifty feet above the deck and striking violently against the spread of the lower rigging rebound

DY'E MIND THE ROLL SHE GAVE.

DINNER TIME AT SEA.

overboard with a plunge to sink from sight instantly and forever'.

At 11 am the cooks of the messes of the watch below went to get up spirits. At 11.30 the pipe was 'clear up decks'; work stopped, and woodwork and bright work given a final clean and polish. At 11.45 the cooks were piped to the galley and at 12 hands were piped to dinner. The food in a Victorian battleship was generous in quantity, if sometimes variable in quality. The full ration scale, per man, per day, was 1¼ lbs. of biscuits or soft bread; 2oz sugar; 1oz of chocolate (for making cocoa); ¼oz of tea; 1lb of fresh meat and ½lb of fresh vegetables, if procurable; if not, then, on alternate days, 1lb of salt pork and ⅓ pint of split peas, or 1lb of salt beef—and 9oz of flour, ¾oz suet and 1½oz of currants or raisins, all which were normally mixed into a 'duff' pudding and boiled in a cloth.

Almost all the food, whether it was beef, pork, soup or pudding, was boiled on the single large coal-fired galley stove, set on bricks amidships on the maindeck. One side of the stove was for the officers' food, the other for the remaining 650 men in the ship's company. The 'cooks' did little more than carry food to and from the galley stove (an Admiralty Committee in 1870 found that ship's cooks generally knew nothing about cooking in any gastronomic or culinary sense of the word). In harbour, and Victorian warships spent a good deal of time in harbour, bumboats came alongside, from which the sailors could buy extras such as sardines, jam, pickles and other delicacies.

One sailor has left a description of dinner-time in a man-of-war in 1860: 'Fancy to yourself a lower-deck mess-table!—time, a quarter to eight bells in the forenoon—presently is heard the bugle playing up cheerly *The Roast Beef of Old England*, and aft to the galley rush the hands whose turn it is to do duty as cooks to draw the day's allowance of meat.

'It is drawn and on the table, and my messmates sit round, and are soon busily engaged in criticising. No matter for dirty hands or tangled hair: it doesn't do to be particular on board ship. ''What won't poison will fatten,'' is a sea proverb. ''Well,'' says Bill, nicknamed the Calf, ''if that's dinner, God send supper! Here's for a smoke;'' and off he goes. Presently, Joe, who has eaten his share, gets up and, after belching rudely in his neighbour's face, exclaims, ''I'd like to have Mr Somerset (Edward Adolphus, 12th Duke of Somerset, First Lord of the Admiralty, 1859-1861) or whatever they call him, just to taste this here meat; I'm blest if it wouldn't make him stare! Beef, they call it; I'm glad they've found a name for it. It beats the tea, so called. I s'pose the Admiralty gets the pair of 'em cut out by the law of economy, don't they?'' ''Bother the odds,'' says lively Tom Jenkins: ''it'll all fill up.''

In theory, there was a procedure for complaints about the food, which could be taken 'quietly and respectfully' before the officer of the watch. The reality, as the same sailor remarked, was somewhat different. 'Some officers,

26

A popular view of Jolly Jack ashore; from "Army and Navy Drolleries", by Captain Seccombe, c1870.

after looking at the faulty article, which is perhaps an eight-pound lump of salt meat, looking similar to a lump of mahogany, will tell you blandly, "he sees no fault in it; very nice meat—very nice indeed; shouldn't wish to eat better himself;" while his countenance belies his words, and he wishes he couldn't smell'.

Sailors were, of course, inveterate complainers and traditionally suspicious of those who fed them and paid them. One Victorian sailor, who lay dying in the Sick Bay, asked as his last wish that the Paymaster and the Ship's Steward be sent for and sit one on each side of his cot while he passed away. However, the sailor recovered and when he was asked the reason for his unusual request said that he felt he could not do better than follow the example of Jesus Christ, who died between two thieves.

Grog was served to those entitled at half past twelve: one gill (an eighth of a pint) of rum, or when rum was not available, half a pint of wine, or a pint of beer. The drawing of the spirits was a ceremony, always attended by an officer on duty, the duty petty officer, the duty ship's corporal and the assistant-clerk (who thereby earned himself the traditional nickname of 'Bungs').

Hands fell in again at 1.30pm for afternoon instruction, exercises and work in parts of ships as in the forenoon. At sea, the decks were cleared up at 3.45pm., and supper was at 4.15, followed by evening quarters and then more drills, shifting spars and sails, at 5. In harbour, evening quarters

was at 4, supper at 4.30 and at 5 both watches fell in to furl awnings and coil up ropes.

At 7.30pm it was 'stand by hammocks' and at 8 'clear up main decks'. At 9 pm in harbour, 8.30 at sea, the Commander did his rounds of all parts of the ship, accompanied by the duty Marine Officer, the mates of decks, the master-at-arms and the ship's corporals. Yeoman of stores stood by for rounds in their respective store-rooms. In harbour, sunset was the end of the official day; a musket was fired, the ensign hauled down, icial day: a mustket was fired, the ensign hauled down, and the top-gallant yards struck. 'Pipe down' was at 9.30. What was known as the 'silent hours' then followed, in which the sailors' rest was respected as far as possible: no bugles were sounded and no pipes were made on boatswain's calls.

Watches were four hours long, from 8 pm to midnight (the First watch), midnight to 4 am (Middle watch), 4 am to 8 (Morning), 8 to 12 (Forenoon) and 12 to 4 pm (Afternoon), except that there were two so-called 'dog watches', the 'first dog' from 4 to 6 pm, the second from 6 to 8, to ensure that no man kept the same watch every day.

The dog watches were the traditional time for the sailors to take their recreation, to 'dance and skylark'. The sailors' various 'jewing firms', the tailors, the barbers, the 'snob shop' (cobblers), all plied their trades in the dog watches.

The 'dogs' were also one of the few times when the sailors could smoke. In a Victorian battleship, smoking was severely restricted as to time and place. No smoking was allowed on the messdecks or in the wardroom or gunroom. Officers smoked on the half deck, wardroom officers on the starboard side, junior officers to port. The sailors could smoke, on the upper deck only, between the top gallant forecastle and the waist gangways, in any of their three meal times, and after evening quarters and drills, until pipe down at 9.30.

The sailors smoked only the 'pussers' service issue tobacco, in pipes, or made up into 'pigtail' lengths for chewing. A 'chaw' was as popular as a smoke on the lower deck and spitkids were always strategically placed on the upper deck during the sailors' leisure times. The officers smoked pipes, of service tobacco occasionally mixed with private brands, or cigars, and could usually smoke on deck until 11 pm in harbour, or 10.30 at sea. Cigarettes were still virtually unknown in a man-of-war of the 1860s.

Clothes were washed on Monday and Thursday evening. Hammocks were scrubbed and clean hammocks slung every fortnight, on alternate Mondays. On Thursday afternoons, whenever possible, hands were piped to 'Make and mend clothes'. Sailors still made all their own clothing, except hats and boots. Some were exceptionally skilful with the needle and made not only clothes, but embroideries, tapestries and strikingly realistic pictures of ships in wool and cotton thread. That visitor in Liverpool, whilst extolling the sailor as 'a pattern to all the world in the domestic virtures of tidiness, cleanliness and order' commented that 'he has too, no little fancy for the arts: his paintings and sketches have always the touch of nature, while his samplers and needlework would not disgrace the finest and most delicate fingers. These little ornamental touches you will come upon at every turn, and it is delightful to see how pleasantly, yet not unprofitably, poor "Jack" employs his leisure; indeed, you might have heard many ladies, after inspecting "Jack's" Berlin wool work, expressing their admiration of the speed and neatness of his workmanship'.

Every Friday morning, whether at sea or in harbour, both winter and summer, hands went to quarters to exercise the great guns and to prepare the ship in all respects for battle. Every other Friday, the exercises were given greater realism. The bugle sounded for action without powder: the whole ship's company, every single man on board, was inspected by, and then drilled under, the Captain, then by the Lieutenants in charge of the quarters, and then exercised at boarding with pikes and cutlasses. The ship's fire brigade was exercised, collision mats were got out and positioned over the ship's side, and damaged rigging was repaired and secured. After all which, hands were piped to 'quarters, clean guns'.

On Friday afternoons, all dirty canvas gear such as wind-sails and deck cloths was scrubbed and the booms were cleaned. Saturday was always given over to cleaning ships, guns and arms, and polishing up wood- and bright—work. Sunday was hardly a day of rest. The sailors used to say, with some feeling (and some justification), 'six days shalt thou labour and on the seventh work harder than ever'. On Sunday morning, there was Captain's rounds of the ship, followed by divisions on the upper deck, followed by church service. Only from dinner time on Sunday could the sailor feel that his day was now his own.

It was a hard life for all. For a man under punishment, one of the so-called 'black list men', it was almost intolerably hard. His whole daily routine was so designed as to remind him constantly that he was in trouble—having to rise earlier and turn in to his hammock later, turn to for work earlier and secure later, work or drill whilst everybody else was off duty. Sometimes punishments took the form of stoppage of leave, or 'watering of grog', or tedious impositions such as having to march up and down the deck, or stand to attention facing a bulkhead, for hours at a time. A man caught spitting on deck might have to carry a spitkid around his neck. Another, with dirty kit, might have to carry an oar over his shoulder with the offending article tied to it.

Later in the 19th century, the basic daily routine of punishment was refined and codified into the dreaded 10A punishment, awarded for seven or fourteen days at a time, which included stoppage of rum and leave, stoppage of smoking, earlier rising and later turning in, extra work and drill, all meals having to be taken on the upper deck under the supervision of a sentry, and hours of standing to attention facing the bulkhead. (This latter punishment, known as 'keeping the flies off the paint-work', survived

until as late as 1912).

The first investigation of an offence was made by the officer of the watch or the duty officer of the day who would expect in the most trival matter refer the case to the Commander, who held his 'defaulters' on the upper deck every working day at 11.30. More serious offences would be referred to the Captain.

Serious offences, incurring more serious punishment, required a 'warrant', in which the Captain set out the circumstances of the offence and the punishment ordered, for transmission to the Admiralty in due course. In *Warrior's* first commission there were 650 men liable to punishment by warrant: 528 seamen, stokers and idlers, and 122 Marines. According to the ship's log, 161 warrants were read, the first being read on 1 April 1862 and the last on 2 December 1863.

The reading of a warrant was itself a solemn ceremony, designed to impress upon the offender and his mates the gravity of the offence. The ship's company were piped to fall in. The offender, with every eye upon him, and trying to appear outwardly nonchalant whilst inwardly quaking, was marched in between two sentries, and stood in front of the assembled ranks while the Captain read out the appropriate Article of War covering the offence and the sentence imposed, after which the offender was wheeled away to undergo or to begin his punishment.

The nature of the warrant offences in *Warrior* is not recorded, but she would be no different from all the other ships in the Navy, in which case the root cause of almost every offence would be drunkenness. Certainly, almost all the offences seem to have been committed in harbour, when leave would be given and liquor would be more readily available.

The number and frequency of warrants decreased markedly towards the end of the commission, suggesting that the ship's company settled down as time went on and gave much less trouble. But the reduction in warrants might also have been the result of the different personalities of the two admirals, first Robert Smart and then Sydney Dacres, who commanded the Channel Squadron during the commission. Smart was known as a martinet. The *United Service Magazine*, which scrutinised ships' punishment returns closely, and commented upon individual serving officers with a freedom which would be impossible today, notes that Rear Admiral Robert Smart 'is said to bear such a name at Plymouth, that he would not be able to get his flagship manned at that port'.

Flogging was still permissible as a punishment, for offences such as habitual drunkenness *at sea*, and acts of insubordination, but it was inflicted far less often, and its use was much more circumscribed, than in the past. A Captain could not order more than four dozen lashes on his own authority. He could not order a flogging until at least twenty-four hours after the offence. He could not order a flogging for a petty officer, a Marine non-commissioned officer, a leading seaman, a man wearing a good conduct badge, or a man in the first class for leave. Two seamen were flogged in *Warrior's* first commission, both on the same day, one receiving four dozen lashes and the other three dozen, for theft. The boys were caned, with their trousers on, or, for more serious offences, birched with their trousers off.

The trend in the Victorian Navy, as in society ashore, was away from corporal punishment, though that remained an option, and towards custodial sentences, in ships' cells, which *Warrior* had on board, or in such establishments as the naval prison at Lewes, in Sussex, when the ship was at Portsmouth, or Dorchester Goal when at Portland. Cell regimes were rigorous. Prisoners lay on hard boards with no blanket except in cold weather, ate bread and water, and had to pick at least two pounds of oakum in a day, as well as undergoing periods of arduous drill. There were some sailors, especially of the old school, who much preferred a flogging. At least it was over and done with and then forgotten.

Warrior's iron hull allowed much heavier guns to be mounted. Her immediate battleship predecessors had virtually reached the limit of the armament which could be carried in a flexible wooden hull. The *Duke of Wellington* Class, for instance, (the name ship, with *Marlborough, Royal Sovereign* and *Prince of Wales*) of wooden screw battleships were some 6,000 tons, could do over 12 knots and mounted no less than 131 guns on three decks. Of those, 16 were 8 in. 65 cwt. shell guns, and 114 were 6 in. bore 32-pounders, with one 8 in. 95 cwt. 68-pounder firing solid shot. The effective range of their broadsides was between 1,000 and 2,000 yards.

The basic philosophy of *Warrior's* gunnery tactics was the same as her predecessors' and indeed the same as in Nelson's day: to get as close alongside an enemy as possible and fire into her 'as fast as she could suck it'. The total weight of *Warrior's* full broadside of thirteen 68-pounders and six 110-pounders (two of the 110-pounders could fire either side) of 1,484 lbs was actually less than the 1,600 lbs full broadside fired by her 131-gun predecessors. But one 68-pound shot had the destructive force of five 32-pound shot and 110-pound shot was equivalent to seven 32-pound shot. So *Warrior's* broadside had the effective power of 3,500 lbs from smaller guns.

ILLUSTRATED LONDON NEWS, 12TH APRIL 1873

The Royal Naval Artillery Volunteers at Exercise

The maximum accurate range of *Warrior's* guns was about 3,000 yards—only 1½ miles. Firing solid shot, with a 16-pound powder charge giving a muzzle velocity of 1,280 feet/sec., the table of elevations and ranges for one of *Warrior's* 68-pounder smooth bore muzzle loader guns was:

Elevation	½°	1°	3°	6°	10°	15°
Range (yards)	340	640	1,400	2,180	2,880	3,620
Time of flight (secs)	½	1½	4	7	11	15

A similar table for a 110-pdr. Armstrong breech loading. gun, using solid shot and a 12-pound charge, was:

Elevation	0°41'	1°26'	3°37'	6°1'	7°58'	10°37'
Range (yards)	300	600	1,400	2,200	2,800	3,600
Time of flight (secs)	1	1.96	4.7	7 57	9.83	12.54

Working the great guns in *Warrior* was extremely labour-intensive. Manning both broadsides (very rarely undertaken—one side only would be much more usual) would take most of the ship's company. There was a Lieutenant as Officer of the Quarters, to supervise the firing. Each gun's crew was under a Petty Officer or a Sergeant RMA, as Captain of the Gun, No.1, who would prime, aim and fire the gun.

No.2, the Second Captain of the Gun, would assist the Captain of the Gun with the breech lever (on a breech-loader), which was heavy enough to require the efforts of two men; he was also responsible for handling the elevating screw, the lock and for cocking the gun. Nos 3 and 4, the Vent Piece Men, removed and replaced the vent-piece which weighed 136 lbs Nos 5 and 6, the Loaders, rammed the 110 lb projectile in place and inserted the powder charge. All these Numbers on the gun would be *Excellent*-trained seamen. The powdermen would bring the cartridge bags containing the powder on their shoulders from the magazine handling hatch to Nos 5 and 6.

The total number in the crew would be 18, most of them being needed for their sheer muscle power, to carry out the basic procedures of serving guns which weighed 95 cwt. (68-pdrs) and 85 cwt. (breech-loaders). The guns were fitted with rear chock carriages, to reduce the recoil, in which the rear wheels of the normal truck carriage were replaced by a heavy chock of wood. They were elevated (maximum 15°) or depressed (maximum 7°) by driving in or withdrawing a quoin (wedge) under the breech, for the 68-pdrs, or by the elevating screw, for the breech-loaders.

They were trained, again by hand, with hand-spikes and by hauling on rope tackles. For loading, the muzzle-loaders were run inboard and the barrels loaded, down the muzzle, with a cartridge bag, shot and wad, in that order, and all well rammed home with the rammer.

The breech-loaders were loaded by turning the two large handles at the rear of the gun, to unscrew the rear end of the breech and allow it move back about an inch. This freed the inner vent piece which could then be lifted out. The shell and cartridge were pushed into the breech, the vent piece replaced, and the two handles turned to tighten the screw.

The arcs of fire were naturally restricted by the widths of the gun-ports. Originally, *Warrior* was to have had gunports 4ft 6ins wide and 3ft 10in high, big enough to permit arcs of 80° (40° each way). But tests showed that, with this size of port, a normal rear chock gun carriage, pivoted two feet from the ship's side, could only achieve an arc of 26° each way. There were advantages in smaller gun-ports. The smaller the gun-ports, the stronger would be the hull and the more protection for the guns' crews. It was found that by siting the gun carriages on a pivot bar, pivoted on the outboard ledge of the lower sill of the gun-port, the outer width of the ports could be reduced to two feet, which gave training arcs of 26° each way (i.e a total arc of 52°). The final height of the gun-ports was 3ft 7¼ins.

The standard solid spherical shot fired by the 68-pdr muzzle loading smooth bores were stowed in racks on the main and lower decks, and *Warrior* carried about 600 of them. Replacements for shot taken from the racks were stowed below in shot lockers beside the cable lockers. There were painted red and, because their diameter was critical, had to be examined for rust or paint thickness before use. Their official diameter was 7.92in., to fit a bore of 8.12in., thus allowing a 'windage' gap of 0.1in each side of the shot; 'windage' was large enough to allow the shot to be loaded easily but narrow enough to prevent too much of the explosive gases escaping when the gun was fired. The official weight of 68lbs actually varied according to the material: cast iron, 67 lbs., wrought iron, 72lbs., steel, 72lbs., chilled steel, 68lbs.8ozs.

The 68-pdrs also fired spherical shell (painted black to distinguish them from solid shot). These were also of 7.92in. diameter, but weighed 47lbs. and were filled with powder to give a total weight of nearly 61lbs. They had a wooden or brass fuse, with its centre filled with combustible material screwed into the shell. The fuse was ignited by the firing of the shell and its length decided the time before the shell exploded; ideally the shell was supposed to explode just before impact. The shell had a wooden plug to ensure that the fuse was always pointing outboard when the shell was loaded. If the shell rotated in the barrel after it was fired, the fuse would be driven into the powder and the shell would explode inside the barrel.

The earlier wooden fuses were gradually replaced in the Navy by brass Moorsom's or Boxer's fuses (named after their inventors). The Boxer's 7½ second fuse had a protective cap which was unscrewed before the shell was rammed down the gun barrel. The fuse was ignited by the explosion of firing the gun and the central combustible material burnt for 7½ seconds until it reached the hole at the base of the fuse and ignited the explosive charge inside the shell.

Officers of HMS Warrior *on deck during her second commission.*

31

The 110-pdr rifled breech loaders fired elongated shot or shells. They were 16 inches long and 7 in diameter to fit the bore, with an outer coating of lead to take up the rifling in the barrel. The elongated shell could either have a time fuse as in the spherical shell, or a percussion fuse in its nose to explode on impact.

Muzzle loaders and breech loaders both had case shot, filled with shrapnel, for use against an enemy crew at close quarters. The breech loaders also had special segmented shells designed to burst into fragments on impact.

Warrior's guns were never fired in earnest, but the crews were thoroughly drilled at least once every week. An allowance of powder and projectiles had to be expended every quarter, a proportion of it being fired off in every month. The guns' crews competed for the best performances every quarter and, every year, to be the best crew in the annual prize firing.

In the stowed or secure position, the gun breeches were lowered so that the muzzles were raised until they rested against the top sills of their gun ports. The guns and their carriages were then securely lashed, to prevent any movement at sea. If a gun and carriage weighing several tons ever came adrift at sea and 'took charge' in a sea-way they could do immense damage to the ship and to other guns and would be a serious danger to the lives and limbs of those trying to secure them.

Clearing for quarters at night, as Captain Cochrane

pointed out, 'meant the men had to leap from their hammocks, stow hammocks, lash tables and benches to the deckhead above, clear away all cooperage, unlash the guns and set them up for firing'. This took more time than usual in *Warrior*—as Captain Cochrane frequently complained, 'the breech of the Gun when secured is so low down between the brackets, that it takes 5 to 6 men to raise the Gun from the housing position, so that a wooden line of Battle Ship ranging alongside at sea, say by night, would open fire from her main Guns for five minutes before it would be possible to get our Guns off. We clear for quarters at night in about 8 minutes, five of which are wasted in raising the breech of the Gun and casting of muzzle lashings, frappings etc . . . '

Ships were inspected by an admiral at least once a year, at irregular times, so that a ship would not have plenty of warning and be able to 'warm the bell' with drills and cleaning. During an inspection in November 1864 by Admiral Seymour, *Warrior's* gunnery was better than Captain Cochrane's somewhat pessimistic comments would suggest. 'Gun crews being in pointed position, they dismounted, shifted carriages across the deck, loaded and fired one round, in the following times: 1st Gun in 3 min. 15 sec., 2nd Gun in 3 min. 16 sec., 3rd Gun in 4 min. 0 sec., and 4th Gun in 4 min. 0 sec. (the 3rd and 4th Guns had had to be lifted over the main anchor cables which ran along the main deck).'

The report for that inspection noted that *Warrior's* gun

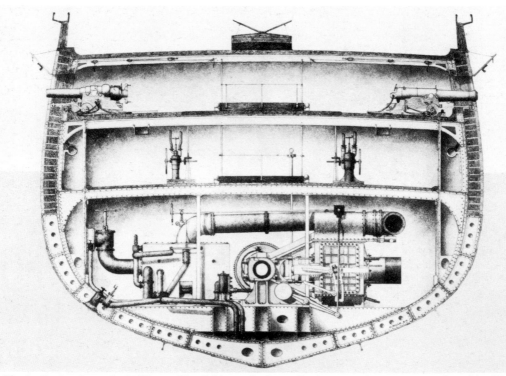

The Warrior *Engine drawn by William Milln, R.N., an Assistant Engineer 1st class, serving on board in 1861.*

crews 'Transported Pivot Gun Forecastle to Stern Port, (a distance of approximately 350ft) and fired one round there 6 min. 30 sec.' Also 'Guns extreme trained (i.e. trained to their maximum degree aft). All laid for an 'enemy' coming up on the Quarter. Order given 'enemy coming down on the bows' (i.e. guns had to be trained the maximum degree forward). Guns relaid in 40 seconds.'

In the days of sail, the captains of guns looked along the muzzles and fired at what they could see. In *Warrior*, sighting the gun was the most important part of the Captain of the Gun's duty and much care was devoted to the gun-sights. The 68-pdrs had six-sided adjustable brass rear sights, with graduations for degrees and for the ranges of the different charges of shot and shell—Distant, Full and Reduced. The Armstrong breech-loaders had elaborate double rear sights with range markings for the various projectiles, and they could be raised or lowered into sockets in the barrel. Small deflections were corrected by the horizontally sliding ''V'' sight. The fore sight was placed halfway along the gun barrel. The guns were actually fired either by detonating tube and hammer, or by friction tube and firing lanyard.

Round and elongated shot were both stored in garlands on the lower and main decks. Shot was replaced from shot lockers amidships. They were in the form of vertical shafts

reaching down into the ship, with iron ladder rungs on one side and shelves on the other. As each shelf was emptied it folded back to reveal the next shelf lower down. Filled round and elongated shells were stored in central shell rooms from where they were hauled up by tackle and carried by hand to the guns.

It seems that originally *Warrior* and *Black Prince* were to have fired shells filled with molten iron. A small iron smelting 'cupola' furnace and fan were fitted at the forward end of the forward stokehole. It is possible that the scheme was short-lived, and the equipment may indeed never have been fitted. Red hot roundshot had been used in naval engagements, especially by the French. But molten iron would have been a very dangerous commodity, even in an iron-hulled ship.

Old timers amongst the guns' crews were surprised and pleased by the speed with which the thick choking smoke produced by the guns cleared from the main deck. Special arrangements were fitted for ventilation. Air was drawn down, through a ventilator on the upper deck, to a steam-powered fan below, between the engine room and the boiler room.

The fan forced air up through a large central trunking, from which it was led through a system of trunkings, port and starboard, throughout the length of the ship,

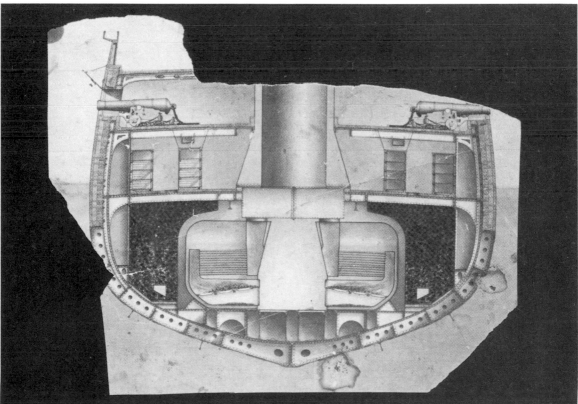

Salvaged from her first captains personal papers. Warrior's **mid-ship section through the boiler room.**

In the engine-room of HMS Warrior, 1860.

providing fresh air to all compartments on the main and lower decks. But at General Quarters (Action Stations) this air was diverted into a number of vertical trunks, each of which had openings or louvres, placed at intervals along the length of the main deck within the citadel.

When the citadel doors were shut, as they were at Action Stations, the air could only escape through hatchways or gratings left open in the upper deck above—or through the open gun ports. Therefore any smoke around the guns was soon whisked away through the ports. Air could also be diverted downwards to ventilate empty coal bunkers if necessary.

However, unlike many other Victorian ironclads, *Warrior* did not have iron (and therefore hollow) lower masts, which were used as ventilation ducts to carry air below. One inspection report noted that *Warrior* was 'not so well ventilated below as some other ironclads, in consequence of not having iron (lower) masts. She has nearly always a large number (30—50) on the sick list than any other ship in the squadron'.

Special arrangements were also made for the storage and handling of powder in the magazines. There were two magazines, one forward and one aft. The after magazine,

which still survives, is a 'hanging' compartment, being suspended away from the ship's side and is divided into two, port and starboard, either side of the propellor shaft.

Men stationed at each deck level carefully handed up the leather cartridge cases full of powder, through hand-up holes, to the two supply scuttles in the main deck, where the powdermen collected them and took them to the guns. They had to be supplied at a rate of 15 to 18 cartridges per minute per supply scuttle, to keep all the guns provided. With two magazines, this meant cartridges were supplied at the rate of 60 per minute. Empty cartridge cases were dropped down through a canvas shute, to arrive at the magazine entrance. From there they were passed by hand through ports in the bulkhead into the magazine to be refilled.

All the fitments in the magazines were of brass. The powder bags were kept in brass cases, nine to a case. The floor of the entrances was sheet lead. The magazines could only be entered through doors on the lower deck and then down through hatches. All hatches and doors were secured at Action Stations. Lighting was from galleries lined with copper, running the lengths of the magazines, in which oil lamps set on brackets shone through sealed glass ports into the magazines. Ventilation was by a hand-operated fan on the lower deck.

The magazines were also inspected during the annual admiral's inspection. Admiral Dacres, in October 1962, noted that 'The crown of the magazine would in my opinion be better protected from vertical fire by stowing thereon bags, hammocks, sails or cables, wetted before going into action, than by the present plan of (water) tanks.' But it seems this suggestion was never carried out. An entry of May 1863 in the Ship's Book noted that 'The whole of the fresh water carried by this ship is stowed on the crown of the fore magazine, and it does not appear that any better arrangements can be made'.

Admiral Dacres inspected the ship again in 1863, when Jackie Fisher was Gunnery Lieutenant. Fisher, who had a strong streak of native cunning himself, always welcomed what would now be called 'one-upmanship' by a member of the ship's company. The chief gunner's mate, Abraham Johnson, came to Fisher beforehand and told him he knew Admiral Dacres and asked Fisher to let him have a free hand.

When the Admiral reached the entrance to a magazine and prepared to come down, Johnson, who was already down in the compartment, called up 'Beg pardon, sir! you can't come down here!' 'Damn the fellow,' said the Admiral, 'what does he mean?' Johnson said again, 'You can't come down here, sir.' 'Why *not?*' demanded the Admiral. 'Because no iron instrument is allowed in the magazine, sir'. '*Ah!*' said the Admiral, unbuckling his sword, '*that* fellow knows his duty! This is a *properly* organised ship!'

The whole of *Warrior's* ship's company must have been delighted by that remark.

Warrior's
Engine Room 1860.

4

Decline and Decay

In 1864, *Warrior* began a long and leisurely refit, lasting until 1867, during which she was completely re-armed. She emerged with 24 guns, twelve a side, in the maindeck citadel. They were, from forward to aft: four 7" 6½—ton Muzzle Loading Rifled (MLR) guns, two 8" 9-ton MLRs, and six 7' 6½-ton MLRs. On the upper deck were another eight 7" MLRs, and four 20-pdr. BLR saluting guns. She was officially designated as a 32-gun ship (the saluting guns being disregarded).

Warrior recommissioned under Captain John Corbett at Portsmouth on 1 July 1867, with *Black Prince's* crew. She was to have been flagship at Queenstown, but this was cancelled almost at once. After one short shake-down cruise, *Warrior* took part in the Fleet Review at Spithead on 17 July in honour of the visiting Sultan of Turkey and the Khedive of Egypt. There was an awe-inspiring array of ships, the greatest display of naval might ever held, but the occasion was almost completely ruined by a sudden summer gale. *Warrior* was then paid off again on 24 July. Captain Corbett and the crew were transferred to the new flagship at Queenstown, the large wooden screw frigate *Mersey*.

On 25 July 1867 *Warrior* commissioned for the third time, for service in the Channel Squadron, under Captain Henry Boys. *Warrior* was not now the novelty she had once been. She could still turn heads and attract attention wherever she appeared, on the sheer magic of her name, and there could only ever be one *Warrior*. But now there were other, newer iron warships. *Warrior* settled down to a somewhat humdrum existence in the Channel Squadron, cruising to the Tagus, and to Queenstown and Belfast, but dividing most of her days between Spithead, Portland and Plymouth.

There had been outbreaks of Fenian activity in 1867. From 28 December 1867 until the following 22 February, *Warrior* stayed at anchor in Cowes Roads, rowing daily guard boats off Queen Victoria's residence at Osborne, on the Isle of Wight. In April 1868, *Warrior* escorted the Royal Yacht *Victoria and Albert*, with the Prince of Wales on board, from Holyhead to Dublin and back.

On 14 August, *Warrior* left Portland with the rest of the Channel Squadron for a cruise, initially to Lough Foyle, Northern Ireland. On the first night at sea, with the weather stormy and visibility poor in rain squalls, the fleet was off the Eddystone Light, heading west for the Scillies,

in open order with double reefed sails in a strong port beam wind. *Warrior's* next ahead was *Royal Oak*, about two points (23°) on *Warrior's* lee bow.

At about 10.45pm, *Royal Oak* was caught aback by a sudden squall, luffed across *Warrior's* bows, and lost way, coming virtually to a standstill in front of *Warrior*. Captain Boys did his best to avoid collision. He ordered mizzen and main topsails backed, the engines full astern, and the helm put hard down, to try and pass to leeward of *Royal Oak*. But *Warrior* was always slow in paying off under sail and had too much way on. Her port bow crashed into *Royal Oak's* starboard lee quarter and ground along her starboard side for some distance, carrying away her starboard quarter boats and wrecking the starboard main and mizzen chains and rigging.

Warrior herself had her flying jibboom, jibboom, buskin and port anchor stocks carried away, and her magnificent figurehead crashed on to *Royal Oak's* quarterdeck (where *Royal Oak's* officers immediately claimed it as a trophy). But she dropped clear at 11pm, stopped engines, made sail again as before, and carried on with the cruise. *Royal Oak* went to Plymouth for repairs.

In the mid—1860s the Admiralty decided to have a large dry dock in the Naval Base at Bermuda. Because the local stone was judged to be too porous, a floating dock was built on the Thames, and completed in May 1869. The 8,200 ton floating dock was to be towed out to her station. Because bad weather might make it necessary to put into a foreign port on passage, the dock was actually commissioned as HMS *Bermuda*, with a Staff Commander in command and ship's company of 82.

Two of the Black Fleet, *Agincourt* and *Northumberland*, towed the dock from the Nore to Porto Santo, Maderia, where they arrived on 4 July 1869. They handed over the tow to *Warrior* and *Black Prince*, who had arrived the day before, and sailed again that same evening of 4th.

It was a strange-looking procession: *Warrior* and *Black Prince* ahead, then *Bermuda*, and, bringing up the rear, and acting as a rudder, the paddle frigate *Terrible* (the largest-ever paddle-wheeled warship in the Navy) and the tender *Lapwing*. However the tow, over a total distance of some 4,000 miles, went almost without incident and was accomplished at an average speed of nearly 5 knots. *Bermuda* arrived off Bermuda on 29 July and was handed over to local vessels. *Warrior* and *Black Prince* stayed only

July 1869—The floating dock HMS Bermuda *under tow from Porto Santo. HM Ships* Warrior *and Black Prince* leading.

Campbell's Patent Floating Dry Dock. An early drawing shows the Warrior *docked without the Caissions.*

Warrior's **figurehead pre 1873.**

forty-eight hours and then returned directly to Plymouth Sound, arriving on 23 August. In September, *Warrior* went to Portsmouth for a docking. A new figurehead was fitted on 8th, (presumably to replace the one damaged in collision with *Royal Oak*).

In October 1869, *Warrior* sailed on an extended cruise with the Channel Squadron, to Lisbon, the Azores, Gibraltar, Teneriffe, and Vigo Bay. She did not return to Spithead until 6 June 1980, after a cruise of 7½ months, the longest period she was ever away from the United Kingdom. In the autumn, *Warrior* was present at the scene of one of the Victorian Navy's greatest tragedies.

On 2 September 1870, *Warrior* was part of a joint Channel and Mediterranean Fleet which sailed from Vigo Bay, for a cruise off the Iberian coast. It was a formidable fleet, of twelve battleships: *Lord Warden* (flag of Admiral Sir Alexander Milne, C-in-C Mediterranean), *Caledonia* (Rear Admiral), *Bellerophon*, *Prince Consort*, *Royal Oak*, *Minotaur* (Vice Admiral Sir Hastings Yelverton, commanding the Channel Squadron), *Agincourt*, *Warrior*, *Northumberland*, *Hercules*, *Monarch* and *Captain*. There were also two frigates, *Bristol* and *Inconstant*, and the tender *Columbine*.

On 6 September, off Cape Finisterre, Admiral Milne transferred to HMS *Captain*, another battleship in his Sub-Division (the other two were *Royal Oak* and *Prince Consort*). *Captain*, the newest addition to the Fleet, had only been in commission a short time. Milne had heard a lot about her and, like the rest of the Navy, he was very curious to see her.

Captain was the brainchild of Captain Cowper Coles, the principal and most persuasive advocate of the turret ship. Coles believed that warships should have a low freeboard, to make smaller targets, and have their guns mounted in turrets outside their hulls. The Admiralty conceded much of the case for turret ships, but deeply mistrusted Cowper Coles' own design. Eventually, after a great deal of pressure from Coles, his friends and supporters and *The Times*, the Admiralty took the unprecedented step of commissioning a ship of Coles' design, and even gave her the famous name, with resonances of Nelson, of *Captain*.

As *Captain* neared completion at Cammell Lairds, a private shipyard, not even Cowper Coles could say she was beautiful. In fact, she looked distinctly odd. She had no upper deck in the conventional sense, but had a sort of flying deck running over the two turrets to connect forecastle and poop. She was awkward and uncomfortable to work and live in. There seemed no proper room for anything or any space to do anything properly.

Fully loaded, *Captain* drew two feet more than designed so that her freeboard was only 6½ feet. Even though she had engines and two propellor shafts, the Admiralty insisted that every ship should also be able to keep its place in the fleet under sail. On top of *Captain's* low ugly hull and her two gun turrets. Coles added the maximum standard spar and sail plan as for a first rate ship. The three masts could not be normally stayed with the usual rigging, which would have interfered with the gun firing arcs. So tripod masts were fitted, adding to the top weight and the wind resistance. It seemed that everything conspired to make *Captain* top-heavy and cranky.

There were plenty of detractors to mutter that *Captain*

HMS Captain *in an Atlantic gale before she foundered in the Bay of Biscay Sept. 1870.*

looked unstable, but her first Captain, Hugh Burgoyne VC, said he was satisfied with her and certainly she rode out a full gale off Ushant with no apparent difficulty. Admiral Milne cast a critical eye on her sailing and handling qualities during his day on board. When, towards evening, the wind began to freshen and Burgoyne urged the Admiral to stay for dinner, Milne insisted on returning to *Lord Warden*. By then, *Captain's* lee rails were awash and Milne got into his boat drenched to the skin. He eventually arrived back on board his flagship saying 'Thank God!'.

The wind continued to strengthen. Upper sails were furled and topsails double reefed, but by 11pm station-keeping was no longer feasible and the flagship signalled 'Open order'. *Captain* acknowledged this signal. At about midnight there was a sharp fierce squall. Every ship in the squadron lost sails or had rigging damaged. It seems that this squall turned *Captain* over. She capsized and sank. Burgoyne and 472 of *Captain's* people were lost. Also drowned was Cowper Coles who was a passenger on board.

Nobody saw *Captain* sink, but at dawn there could be no doubt of her fate and the fleet spread out for 15 miles to look for her. Soon various ships began to report wreckage. The frigate *Psyche* joined the fleet on 7 September reporting that she had 'passed cutters bottom upwards, with spars'. At 5.10am on 8th, according to the log kept by a Navigating Midshipman on board, *Warrior* lowered cutter, picked up 2 boat's brakers, oars, smaller pieces of wreck, pendulum, 1 half post and capstan bar of HMS *Captain*.' *Warrior* lowered more boats later to pick up 'some floating wreck, boat's gear etc.', 'hatch ladder' and 'part of hammock netting'.

On 9 September, the frigate *Volage* joined the fleet with Gunner May and 17 sailors who had got ashore in a launch. These were the only survivors from *Captain*. Milne made a general signal 'Admiral is sure all will sympathise with regard to the dreadful disaster that has occurred'.

The dramatic circumstances of *Captain's* loss quite obscured the excellence of the Admiralty's own design of turret ship, HMS *Monarch*, who was present that day off Finisterre. *Monarch*, designed by Edward James Lyon, the Chief Constructor, was the first ocean-going warship to embody all three great advances in Victorian fighting ship design—to fight under steam instead of sail, to be built of metal and not timber, and to have her main armament outside rather than inside her hull. *Monarch* was faster than *Captain* under steam and at every point of sailing, had a smaller turning circle, could fire her guns in much heavier weather and, in short, was superior to *Captain* in every respect.

Almost a year later, on 1 July 1871, *Warrior* was present at another contretemps when *Agincourt* ran aground on the Pearl Rock as the fleet was steaming west out of Gibraltar. *Warrior* herself was only 2½ cables (500 yards) astern of *Agincourt*, and had to go full speed astern and hard a starboard to avoid a similar fate. *Agincourt* was stuck fast and might have become a total loss but fortunately the sea was calm. For three days, *Warrior* and the other ships sent large working parties of sailors across to *Agincourt* to remove her guns and other weights into lighters sent out from Gibraltar.

But *Agincourt* refused to move. At last, *Hercules* was ordered to assist and succeeded in towing *Agincourt* clear. *Warrior's* sailors, like the rest of the fleet, manned the rigging and cheered when *Agincourt* was finally seen to be underway. *Agincourt* herself was found to be not much damaged, but both admirals concerned were superseded.

HMS *Agincourt* aground on the Pearl Rock— Gibraltar Bay.

On 6 August, *Warrior* sailed from Vigo as part of what was almost certainly the most powerful British fleet ever seen at sea up to that time. In all there were 23 major warships, from the Channel and Mediterranean Fleets, the 1st Reserve Squadron, and the Flying Squadron, formed in three lines of columns of divisions in line ahead:

Starboard Division	Centre Division	Port Division
(1st Reserve Squadron)	**(Flying Squadron)**	**(Channel Sqdn. & Med. Flt.)**
Achilles **(Senior Officer)**	*Narcissus* **(flag)**	*Lord Warden* **(Flag of V-Adm Sir Hastings Yelverton, C-in-C, Med. Flt.)**
Black Prince	*Cadmus*	*Hercules* **(Channel)**
Resistance	*Immortalité*	*Monarch* **(Channel)**
Invincible	*Topaze*	*Prince Consort* **(Med.)**
Repulse	*Volage*	*Northumberland* **(Channel)**
Hector	*Inconstant*	*Defence* **(Med.)**
Valiant		*Caledonia* **(Med.)**
Penelope		*Warrior* **(Channel)**

But this was *Warrior's* last appearance in such grand company. On 1 September 1871, she arrived alongside Island Jetty, Portsmouth, to dismantle the ship, hoist out masts, guns and carriages. On 12th, she moved to Pitch House Jetty and on 15 September her log recorded again 'Sunset. Hauled down the pendant'. This was the end of *Warrior's* service as a first line warship. She was paid off into the 4th Division of the Reserve and during the next 3½ years underwent a second major refit, in which she was reboilered, with similar boilers but with superheaters added. A poop was fitted aft, and her forward capstan coverted to steam operation.

Warrior recommissioned, under Captain William H Whyte, at Portsmouth on 1 April 1875, for second-line service in the 1st Reserve. For the rest of her sea-going life she was to be what was known as the District Ship, for Coastguard and Royal Naval Reserve duties, at Portland until 1 May 1881 and then until 1 June 1883, when her sea-going was finally over, at Greenock.

The first Reserve Squadron normally went on a summer cruise every year. In her first such cruise, *Warrior* was present at another Victorian Navy mishap. Ever since the Austrian flagship *Erzherog Ferdinand Max* rammed and sank the Italian ironclad *Re d' Italia* at the battle of Lissa in 1866, the ram had been highly regarded as a weapon in fleet actions. But in peacetime the ram was like a weapon kept permanently cocked against friends. Every ship in company was always threatened by her next astern.

In July 1875, after complaints from Irish Members of Parliament that Ireland did not see enough warships, seven ironclads of the Reserve Squadron embarked 'fleetmen', or reservists, and sailed under Vice Admiral Sir John Walter Tarleton, flying his flag in *Warrior*, for a six-week training and flag-showing cruise right round Ireland. They intended to visit half a dozen ports, finishing at Dublin.

On 1 September, Tarleton still had a small squadron under his command, of *Warrior*, *Hector*, and the sister ships *Iron Duke* and *Vanguard*. The four ships sailed from Queenstown for exercises that morning, but when they were off the Kish Light and just changing station on the flagship, they ran into fog so thick that no ship could see any other. Unfortunately *Vanguard* suddenly sighted a small sailing vessel close under her starboard bow and altered sharply to port to avoid it.

Iron Duke, who should have been directly astern, was instead some distance out of station to port. *Vanguard* thus unwittingly turned right across *Iron Duke's* bows. *Iron Duke's* ram struck *Vanguard* a fatal blow on her port side amidships, flooding her engine room and boiler rooms. Efforts were made to pump out the water but after about two hours, *Vanguard* sank stern first in 100 feet of water, leaving the tops of her masts showing.

All her ship's company were picked up and no lives were lost. But *Vanguard's* captain, Captain Richard Dawkins, was severely (and quite unjustifiably) reprimanded by the court martial, dismissed his ship and never employed again. The verdicts aroused much bad feeling in the fleet, on the lower deck and in wardrooms. Several scurrilous songs about the Admiralty were composed and sung for some years.

Warrior returned to her usual station at Portland, where Tarleton struck his flag, and *Warrior* resumed her somewhat humdrum existence in the Reserve—as a 'Gobby Ship', as they were disrespectfully called. 'Gobby Ships' were not sought after appointments. They normally only had half complements, and went to sea for only one day a quarter to carry out quarterly firing practise. They also had an annual spring docking, which in *Warrior's* case was usually at Portsmouth.

Gobby Ships' complements were made up to strength with additional personnel only for the annual summer cruises. *Warrior* took part in every cruise from 1875 to 1882, going to Gilbraltar in 1876, to Vigo in 1877 and in 1878 to Bearhaven, Bantry Bay, in so-called Particular Service Squadron. This was a somewhat motley collection of 16 second-line warships, assembled as part of a general mobilisation because of the Russian war scare of that year. The Squadron was commanded by Admiral Sir Astley Cooper Key, flying his flat in *Hercules*, with Rear Admiral Henry Boys, a previous captain of *Warrior*, as Second in Command— and actually flying his flag in his old ship.

Britains first two ironclads—HMS Warrior (foreground) with HMS Black Prince.

The sinking of HMS Vanguard—*from a sketch by one of her officers.*

Queen Victoria reviewed the Particular Squadron at Spithead on 13 August 1878, when the scare was over and the Squadron was about to disperse. This was the last Review *Warrior* attended, although her sister ship *Black Prince* was present at three more.

The cruise in 1879 was to Gibraltar, Lagos Bay and Vigo. When leaving Portland for the 1880 cruise on 29 June, *Warrior* nudged the breakwater and had to return for a divers' inspection, which showed no damage. She sailed for Plymouth where she went into dock for a more thorough inspection. She embarked 'fleetmen', as the reservists were called, on 5 July and sailed for Torbay to join the rest of the Reserve Squadron on 6th. Next day the Squadron sailed for the annual cruise.

Taking part that year were four ironclads of the Channel Squadron, *Minotaur, Agincourt, Northumberland* and *Achilles,* and the Reserve Squadron of nine ironclads, *Hercules* (wearing the flag of 'Affie', now HRH The Duke of Edinburgh), *Warrior, Lord Warden, Hector, Valiant, Belleisle, Penelope, Audacious* and *Defence,* with the tender *Lively.*

These 'fleetmen' cruises were not holiday cruises. Admiral Ballard, who was then in *Achilles,* described what happened between 22 July, when the squadron left Bearhaven, and 31st, when they reached Vigo. They weighed from Bearhaven on a Thursday evening and on getting outside they sent down royal yards and pointed the other yards to the wind. On Friday morning 'they exercised general quarters, and in the evening crossed royal yards, made plain sail, shortened and furled all sail. On Saturday, struck topgallant masts. On Sunday there were

THE BRITISH RESERVE SQUADRON.
AT PORTLAND. JUNE. 1878.

no drills, but the yards were braced round twice to shifts of wind. On Monday the watch was excercised morning and afternoon in shifting main topsail. In the evening they sent up topgallant masts, crossed upper yards, made all plain sail, reefed topsails, shook out reefs, furled sails, sent down upper yards, struck topgallant masts. On Tuesday, the watch exercise was shifting foresail; in the evening hands were exercised at fire quarters, which included getting up the tackles for hoisting out boomboats. On Wednesday they exercised each watch in shifting jibboom, and in the evening sent up topgallant masts, crossed upper yards, made plain sail, furled again. Thursday being small-arm Company day, no watch drills took place aloft; but in the evening hands made plain sail, set stunsails one side, shifted topsails and furled sails. On Friday morning they prepared for action aloft, which meant unbending all square sails, sending topgallant masts, upper yards and stunsail booms on deck, and running bowsprits in. They then exercised general quarters, and after general quarters bent all sails again, sent up all spars that were down, and ran out the bowsprits. On Saturday they moored in Vigo Bay, hoisted out boomboats, and in the evening sent down upper yards.'

In April 1881, *Warrior* exchanged officers and ship's companies with *Hercules* before taking up her new station at Greenock (although she did not actually arrive and moor at the Tail o' the Bank, Greenock, until the beginning of October). The 1881 cruise took *Warrior* further

north than she had ever been before or was ever to go again, to Heligoland (which was then British) and then to the Baltic, to Cronstadt and Kiel. *Warrior's* final cruise, and her last passage outside British waters, was in 1882, to Arosa Bay and Gibraltar, under Rear Admiral HRH The Duke of Edinburgh, who had visited *Warrior* so often as a young midshipman many years before, flying his flag in *Hercules*.

On 8 May 1883, *Warrior* sailed from Greenock for her last sea-going passage under her own power. She anchored at Spithead on 11th, went up harbour for the last time on 14th, and secured alongside the coaling jetty in the Tidal Basin on the following afternoon and spent the next 16 days destoring and dismantling ship. On 31 May, she paid off and the log recorded, for the last time as a sea-going ship, 'Sunset. Hauled down the pennant'. In her 22 years of service, in which she been more than six years in full commission and eight in the First Reserve and had steamed and/or sailed some 90,000 sea miles, *Warrior* had never seen an enemy ship nor ever fired a shot in anger.

From October 1887, *Warrior* was officially designated a 32 Gun Screw Battle Ship, 3rd Class, Armoured. In May 1892, she became a 32 Gun Screw Cruiser, 1st Class, Armoured. At about this time there were suggestions that she should be modernised and rearmed to act as a guardship at one of the numerous coaling stations abroad. But it was decided she was not worth the expense. For nearly twenty years *Warrior* lay neglected, a hulk in everything but name, moored with other derelicts in what was known

H M S WARRIOR
966

In No. 10 Dock at Portsmouth.

45

Rotten Row—Portsmouth Harbour 1899. Warrior *(left),* Resistance *(right).*

as 'Rotten Row' in a remote corner of Portsmouth harbour. Early in 1900, she was officially recognised for what whe had become: 'Only considered available as hulk'.

In 1902, *Warrior* was selected for service as a hulk. She was stripped of her engines and boilers at Southampton, and fitted for her new duties, including more modern water-tube boilers. On 7 July 1902, at Portsmouth, *Warrior* was recommissioned (still under her own name) under Captain John de Robeck as a Stationary Depot Ship for Torpedo Boats and Destroyers. She paid off on 31 March 1904 and her crew were transferred to HMS *Erebus* but recommissioned the next day, 1 April, as a Torpedo School Ship and part of the Torpedo Establishment HMS *Vernon*. At that time the whole establishment was afloat in hulks: *Vernon* (ex-*Donegal*), *Vernon II* (ex-*Marlborough*), and *Vernon III* (ex-*Warrior*). *Warrior's* boilers provided the steam for all three.

While *Warrior* was serving as *Vernon III*, another *Warrior*, an armoured cruiser of 13,550 tons, was launched in 1905. She was armed with six 9.2'' and four 7.5'' guns and had a designed speed of 23 knots. She was in the 1st Cruiser Squadron at Jutland on 31 May 1916, when she was hit and badly damaged, losing all power and suffering some 70 casualties amongst her ship's company. *Defence* and *Black Prince*, *Warrior's* squadron mates, were both sunk in the same engagement. *Warrior* herself was taken in tow by the seaplane tender *Engadine* but had to be abandoned and scuttled, about 160 miles east of Aberdeen.

Vernon became a shore establishment on 1 October 1923, but *Warrior* remained attached for another six months, and finally paid off on 31 March 1924—having thus been part of *Vernon* for exactly 20 years. She had been omitted from the Navy List since 1 October 1923, and was listed for disposal, although she resumed her own name.

It seemed only a matter of time before the hulk was finally scrapped. But *Warrior* was reprieved. On 22 October 1927, she was taken in hand at Portsmouth for conversion to an oil fuel pontoon hulk. What remained of her masts and rigging and much of her upper deck gear was removed. Below, the remains of her boilers and engines was also removed. She became in effect a floating pontoon, empty for all practical purposes, against which other ships could berth.

Warrior was towed to Pembroke Dock, South Wales, to take up her new duties as a floating jetty for oil tankers in March 1929. There she remained, and became a familiar sight in the estuary. For a period in World War Two she was used as a base depot ship for coastal forces. On 27 August 1942, she was officially redesignated yet again, becoming baldly and ignominiously 'Oil Fuel Hulk C.77'. This was to make the name available for another *Warrior*, a 13,000 ton Colossus Class light fleet aircraft carrier launched at Harland & Wolff in May 1944. This *Warrior* was loaned to the Royal Canadian Navy from 1946 to 1948, was the headquarters ship of a Special Service Squadron for the British hydrogen bomb tests at Christmas Island in 1957, was sold to Argentina in 1958 and renamed *Independencia*. She was broken up in 1971.

C.77 survived until long after the Second World War. Her caretaker, Mr James, dispensed warm Welsh hospitality to visitors from his quarters on the poop, where he and his family lived a Peggotty-like existence (their daughter was married from the ship). The name *Warrior* was transferred yet again, to the Headquarters of C-in-C Fleet at Northwood, in Middlesex. In the 1970's the old *Warrior* was about to be towed away for the very last time to be scrapped when it was realised by a few enlightened people that here was the Navy's first ocean-going iron-hulled battleship which had, by a miracle, survived. In August/September 1979, the old ship, once again called *Warrior*, was towed round to Hartlepool. One existence had come to an end. But another was just about to start.

5

New Life

For 50 years Warrior *lay as a hulk at Pembroke Dock. The occasional visiting tanker or warship lying alongside her whilst embarking fuel.*

The idea of saving *Warrior* from the breakers' yard and preserving her for posterity did not appear suddenly overnight. As long ago as 1967, Mr John Smith, the then Conservative Member for the Cities of London and Westminister, was putting parliamentary questions about historic ships such as *Warrior* and *Unicorn* to the Ministry of Education. As a member of the Historical Buildings Council and the National Trust Council, John Smith was concerned with the environment and the national heritage some years before these topics became fashionable.

With a background of Eton and Oxford, wartime service as a RNVR Lieutenant in the Fleet Air Arm from 1942-46, a director of Coutts Bank, an MP, a land-owner and Lord Lieutenant of Berkshire, John Smith was in a position to knock on the right doors and see the right people. It is fair to say, and no exaggeration, that without him *Warrior*

would have been scrapped or, at best, still be a hulk somewhere awaiting preservation some time.

In 1962, John Smith formed the Maniford Trust, an independent fund-raising and grant-making trust to finance environmental projects. As he says, 'houses and ships were our things'. The trust was involved in such diverse projects as the repair of churches, and especially church bells, the Kennet & Avon Canal, the preservation of HMS *Belfast* in the Thames and of ss *Great Britain* at Bristol. But *Warrior* was special. 'If every warship in the 19th Century still existed and was available for preservation,' John Smith said, '*Warrior* would still be my first choice'.

Several proposals for restoring *Warrior* were floated during the 1960's, but none of them came to fruition. The ship was, in any case, still in service at Llanion Cove,

A bare main deck during her time at Pembroke Dock. Note her solid construction—the designer at least intended she would last . . .

The hulk . . . C77 awaiting her fate in 1977.

Pembroke Dock, and thus still required by the Ministry of Defence. In 1967 there was a suggestion by the Greater London Council to use *Warrior,* who had been built on the Thames, as the 'flagship' of a proposed yacht marina at Thamesmead new town, down river from Woolwich. Then it was proposed to place the restored *Warrrior* in the Royal Victoria Docks, in the Borough of Newham. But all such proposals eventually foundered for lack of money. It was already plain that *Warrior's* restoration would cost a prodigious sum.

In March 1976 it was announced that the Llanion Fuel Depot was to close on 1 April 1978, and *Warrior* would no longer be required. In 1977, the Manifold Trust undertook to raise the money for *Warrior's* restoration (estimated even then at £3 million) - with, it was hoped, substantial contributions from other public and private sources.

It was announced in the House of Commons on 12 June 1979 that *Warrior* had been given (actually, free of charge) into the keeping of the Maritime Trust, which had been interested in her preservation and had been trying to find the means to accomplish it for some years. The Maritime Trust had been founded by HRH The Duke of Edinburgh in 1970 to 'restore and put on display ships and equipment of interest and importance in the technical, commercial and military history of this country' - a perfect definition of the philosophy behind preserving *Warrior.*

Warrior would be an important addition to the twenty vessels already owned by the Trust, which included the *Cutty Sark* at Greenwich (the Trust merged with the Cutty Sark Society in 1975), Captain Scott's *Discovery* (taken over from the Royal Navy in 1979) at Dundee, Sir Francis Chichester's *Gypsy Moth IV* and Sir Alec Rose's *Lively Lady.* The Trust had a collection of historic and classic

ships at St. Katharine's Dock, near the Tower of London, which included a coal-fired steam herring drifter, the Thames spritsail barge *Cambria,* an example of a 'dirty British coaster with a salt-caked smokestack', and the Nore Light Vessel.

Warrior was officially handed over to the Trust on 20 August 1979, on the understanding that the Trust would do its best to preserve and restore the ship and eventually open her to the public. For the sake of increased efficiency and convenience in reconstruction and in fund-raising, ownership of *Warrior* was transferred by the Trust to its wholly-owned subsidiary, and, like its parent a registered charity, the Ship's Preservation Trust (renamed the *Warrior* Preservation Trust in 1985) which had been set up for the sole purpose of restoring the ship.

The first major decision was to choose the place where *Warrior* could be restored. A number were considered and the choice eventually came down to two: Falmouth, in Cornwall, and Hartlepool, in Cleveland, in the north-east of England. Both were towns with a ship-building and ship-repairing history, a high rate of unemployment, and a suitable climate. Both towns had considerable reserves of skilled ship-building labour. Hartlepool's case on all these points was probably the stronger but the decisive factor in the end was almost certainly the decision of the Manpower Services Commission to support the restoration as a community project at Hartlepool, and to contribute towards the wages of the labour force, most of whom would be recruited from the locally unemployed. There was also the prospect of substantial grants from the E.E.C., the government and the British Steel Corporation.

On 29 August 1979, *Warrior* was towed out of Milford Haven by the tug *Hendon* and reached Hartlepool on 2

The final preparations are made for the long tow to Hartlepool.

The brow is removed and just one mooring chain remains . . .

Before she is eased from her berth . . .

51

A distinctive 'H' reveals her 'secondary role' as a helicopter landing site whilst at the fuel depot.

A handful of spectators wave farewell to the local landmark.

LT CDR L. PHILLIPS RNR

Hartlepool bound. Warrior still with her sheds and "street lighting" heads for the open sea.

September. She was berthed temporarily in the Union Dock on 3rd, and finally moved to the Old Coal Dock, where she was to be restored, on 7 September.

The ship might be free, but her berth certainly was not. Some £35,000 was spent on dredging the Coal Dock prior to Warrior's arrival and the fee for the berth alongside was £18,000 a year. This had risen to £25,000 in 1985.

The chairman of the Ships Preservation Trust, from its beginnings, was Maldwin Drummond, from Cadland in Hampshire. He joined Warrior in August 1979 (they talk of 'joining' her, as though she were still one of Her Majesty's Ships in commission). One of those public-spirited people prepared to give up his time to sit on committees and on his local magistrates bench, Maldwin Drummond was a very well known personality in business, sailing and nautical circles, and the author of books on ships and the sea. He was on the Council of the Maritime Trust and chairman of the Sail Training Association. The Secretary of the Trust was Vice Admiral Sir Patrick Bayly, Director of the Maritime Trust.

Also on the Trust board were the restoration project manager at Hartlepool, Ray Hockey, and the representative of the Manifold Trust, Tom Dulake, who had much experience of restoration work carried out by the Trust. In 1982, when, to the Manifold Trust's disappointment, no other major source of money nor substantial donor had appeared, control of the project was taken over by the Manifold Trust and Tom Dulake became Managing Director of the Ships Preservation Trust with overall responsibility for the restoration.

The guidelines for the restoration were carefully thought out and far-sighted. Warrior was to be restored to her 1861 appearance, when she was first commissioned. This was an obvious choice because, although she was the last word in 1861, she became obsolescent when Achilles appeared in 1865, and her later career was unremarkable. She was also to be restored to such a condition that she could last another 20 years without further major work. Finally, nothing was to be removed or added which would prevent further restoration, if it should ever be reconsidered at some time in the future.

The work of restoration was first contracted to a Washington-based organisation called Locomotion Enterprises. The project got underway, with high hopes, on 22 October 1979 when the first workforce—foreman Stan Morrell, two shipwrights and five labourers—went on board to start work. At about the same time the Old Custom House, a short distance away from the ship, was acquired for offices.

In March 1980, HRH The Duke of Edinburgh visited Warrior to see for himself how matters were progressing and to give the project a very welcome publicity boost. Two days after the royal visit, Locomotion Enterprises announced they were withdrawing from the project, because of contractual difficulties. Thenceforth, the Ships Preservation Trust itself took over the project.

Two early and important research appointments were John Wells as Research Director and, later, Portsmouth Liaison Officer to Warrior, and Walter Brownlee as Ship's Historian at Hartlepool. John Wells retired from the Royal Navy as a Captain in 1964 (having actually served in the aircraft carrier Warrior as Commander and Executive Officer from 1953-55). A gunnery officer, he was the

John Smith—Without his efforts it is most unlikely Warrior would have been restored.

Walter Brownlee onboard in 1987.

author of a history of HMS *Excellent,* the gunnery branch's alma mater at Whale Island, of which he was once Captain.

Walter Brownlee was a master mariner who, when he came ashore, became a school teacher and headmaster. He was interested in *Warrior* from the moment she arrived in Hartlepool and became involved in her restoration on a part-time basis. But in September 1982 the Cleveland County Education Authority seconded him from his post as Teacher/Warden of Stockton Teachers' Centre to become Education Liaison Officer HMS *Warrior* for two years. In September 1984, his appointment was made permanent. As the official Ship's Historian, he led the Hartlepool-based historical research, reconstruction and record keeping. He also dealt with schools visits and audio visual aids. His chief task was to keep the research ahead of the reconstruction, so that when a particular ship's fitting had to be ordered or made at Hartlepool, plans and drawings were available to show what it looked like.

When *Warrior* arrived in Hartlepool it needed an enthusiastic and a charitable eye to see her graceful and powerful lines. Her black hull was battered and had a broad band, once white but now somewhat stained, running along most of its length. At some time, a ship coming alongside her had knocked off about eight feet of the iron beak, which originally carried her massive figurehead, and torn out her port after hawse-hole. Divers had recovered the damaged beak from the bed of the river estuary and it was still there, covered in barnacles, on the upper deck.

Also on her upper deck were all the fittings left over from her days as C.77; a pair of derricks, a sponson-like structure on the starboard side over which the oil fuel hoses were hauled, lamp-posts for floodlights, two or three wooden cabins, a wooden poop, and a helipad. The seven-foot high bulwarks had long since been removed.

The upper deck was in a very poor state and the first, the longest and the most laborious task of the restoration was to clear, repair and seal it. When all the superfluous 20th Century fitments had been removed, the full effects of more than a hundred years of neglect were laid bare. It seemed that when *Warrior* ceased to be in commission and became a hulk, any worn section of upper deck planking was replaced with whatever wood was available. Later, when she became an oil jetty, rotten parts of the deck were torn up and the whole 400 feet of her upper deck was covered with concrete to a depth of about six inches.

Over the years, this concrete cladding had cracked and allowed water to seep through it, causing rust below. In some places stalactites of lime from the concrete were actually hanging down into the main deck. In May 1980, work began to remove the concrete—some 250 tons of it—with heavy pneumatic drills and hammers. The exposed deck showed a criss-cross pattern of wrought iron strengtheners, pitted with hundreds of old bolt holes and studded with many of the bolts which had once held the deck planking in place.

There were pockets of rust, where the original wrought iron deck had completely corroded away and had to be replaced with steel plates. Until that was done, the upper deck leaked in a hundred places and, when it rained, the main deck below was a wet as the upper deck above.

The work of sealing the upper deck went on through to 1981. By the end of that year, all was sealed except a few square yards in the area of the bows. With the upper deck sealed, the main deck below could begin to dry out. This deck had also been covered to a depth of 1½ inches with an oil proof compound which had to be broken up and removed.

Hundreds of tons of rubbish had to be cleared from the upper and main decks, and properly secured ladders and hand-rails erected. Below, the wrought iron structure of the compartments was found to be in generally good condition. The wrought iron hull itself had hardly admitted more than a teacupful of water (and it was reputed that the only water in the bilges when *Warrior* arrived was fresh).

The work of removing 'rubbish' had to be done with the greatest care. In all the years when *Warrior* had been C.77 and before, nobody had taken any interest in anything below the upper deck after the last *Vernon* classes left. Thus nobody yet knew how much of the original ship still remained and how many of her original fittings and equipment were still on board. That apparently useless hunk of unidentified rusting metal, fit only to be ditched, could well turn out to be—once it was irretrievably gone—part of a priceless, original, irreplaceable Victorian ship's fitting.

One of the first restoration tasks was therefore to examine and record the position of every hole and crevice, every ledge and projection, every telltale sign of where a ship's fitting or an item of equipment might have belonged. Later experience showed how important this precaution was; for example, insignificant fittings on the bulkheads proved to be clips for Colt revolvers. When a Colt revolver was tried in one, it clicked perfectly into place.

When the upper deck had been sealed, only a few blackened and crumbling patches of the original wood remained. Originally the upper deck had been made of 8" x 4" planks, most of them 20 feet long, bolted to the iron deck. The gaps between planks were caulked with oakum and hot pitch. The total area of upper deck was 16,580 square feet, or about the size of six tennis courts, or over a third of an acre.

Such an area of timber would cost an estimated £90,000. However, in 1981, Bradford Corporation contracted with W. Reidy & Son Ltd to demolish an old wool warehouse, built in 1881, which was disused and had become an eyesore. It had five storeys, all floored with 9" planks of Finnish Redwood, each about 3½" thick. Every plank was grooved along its length and locked to its neighbour by galvanised iron strips.

The wood was in prime condition and was bought for £10,000. The first consignment of timbers arrived on the quay beside *Warrior* on 18 November 1981. Thus, by the greatest good fortune, *Warrior* was to be redecked, not with 20th Century timber, but with genuine Victorian

Internally, facilities were somewhat basic—but still intact.

Emergency lights were rigged to enable work below decks to commence. If the light didn't get in—the rain did!

wood from her own contemporaries—mature trees that were growing when she was launched.

The laborious but skilled work of replanking the upper deck began in the spring of 1983, continued through that summer, and was largely finished by November. Channel bars were adzed ('adzing' itself is an almost lost ship-yard skill, resurrected for *Warrior*) from baulks of pitch pine, 1 foot by 1 foot by 12 feet, and then fitted into place along the outer edges of the upper deck, where it met the ship's side. The various hatchway coamings, positioned amidships down the length of the upper deck, were fabricated from timbers, dove-tailed together, and then bolted into position. Later the hatch coaming would have fitted wooden gratings.

The main expanse of the deck to be planked was now defined. Rows of bolts were fastened into the metal deck in the way of the planks. Each deck plank was placed on top of its bolts and the positions of the bolts marked and drilled out. The planks were then laid so that the bolts fitted into their drilled holes. The planks were bolted into place. The bolt-hole recesses were filled with wood dowels, so as to leave a smoothly surfaced deck.

The deck seams were then caulked. Oakum was teased into strands, rolled into lengths like rope and hammered with caulking chisels into the seams between the planks. Hot pitch was poured ('payed', was the old sailors' word) into the seams. Caulking is yet another dying skill, so watching the caulkers at work on *Warrior's* upper deck, with the heavy pungent smell of pine wood and hot tar, and the steady rhythmic thudding of a dozen men pounding their caulking mallets into the seams, was like stepping back into the 19th Century. Behind the caulkers came the men with hot tar, being 'payed' into the seams.

The so-called Devil's Seams—those against hatch coamings and the ship's side—were as awkward as they had been in Nelson's day, and are a possible origin of the phrase 'The devil to pay and no pitch hot' (which generally means that some action is expected or needed but there is nobody to take it). Finally, the deck was machine-planed, to remove tar and other stains and leave fresh, clean wood, with narrow black lines of caulking.

Some of the local reaction to *Warrior's* arrival in Hartlepool was less than ecstatic. There were hostile letters in the local paper calling her 'junk' and suggesting that she could at least fulfil some useful purpose if she were filled with bricks, towed out and sunk as an extra breakwater. There is a certain kind of mentality, which frequently feels it necessary to write to its local newspaper, which assumes that any expenditure must come from 'us the tax payers' or 'us the ratepayers'. The accusation was that *Warrior* was being restored at enormous public expense. This attitude had to be sharply refuted by replies from the Maritime Trust, pointing out that *Warrior's* restoration was a charity undertaking and entirely privately financed.

Much more representative of Hartlepool feeling were the 'Friends of the Warrior', a registered charity formed by a group of local volunteers very soon after *Warrior* arrived,

to support the ship, generate interest in her and raise money for her. The Friends held monthly meetings, arranged social functions, organised lectures and publicity, and manned the Ticket Office and the Souvenir Shop on days when the ship was open to the public.

The Friends took parties on conducted tours round the ship, using their imagination (large quantities of which were needed in the early days) to try and recreate for the visitors a mental picture of the ship as she once was. They continued to do so, with a remarkably stable membership, until the day before *Warrior* sailed, nearly eight years later. Now that *Warrior* has left Hartlepool, the Friends intend to carry on the same service for *Foudroyant* when she arrives.

In July 1983, the Warrior Association, also a registered charity, was formed 'to support the Ship's Preservation Trust (later called the Warrior Preservation Trust) in the reconstruction of HMS Warrior (1860) and her display in Portsmouth in a berth provided by the Portsmouth City Council'. The Association, which is more orientated in membership and activity than the Friends to the south of England, has manned *Warrior* stands at Portsmouth Navy Days, the RNLI Summer Fair at Southsea and the RN Equipment Exhibition at Whale Island. The Association sponsored a successful *Warrior* Fore Topmast Appeal and a *Warrior* Gun Appeal, to raise £3000 to pay for the 110-pounder gun now at the entrance to Portsmouth Naval Base adjacent to *Warrior's* berth.

In the Gun Appeal, contributors could become any member of the guns crew, depending upon the amount they subscribed, from the Gunnery Lieutenant himself (£250, 'for those who want to run the whole shooting match') down to Powder man (£2).

There was, at first, a problem in recreating *Warrior's* great guns. All her own had, of course, long since vanished, as had all the similar 2,000 naval 68-pounders made and used in the 1860s. They had all, it was thought, either been scrapped and melted down, or used for shore defence batteries and had then disappeared. It seemed unlikely that any gun had survived.

But, it appears that there is a Providence which wants *Warrior* to be restored. As it happened, an 1860 68-pounder barrel was found by accident. It was lying in the grass amongst dozens of other barrels outside the main building of the Rotunda Museum, Woolwich.

The barrel had no proof markings and was never issued for service. But it seems it is now the only 68-pounder barrel in existence, and, apart from some numbers and figures which were stamped into the metal and which are missing, it has the same dimensions as *Warrior's* 68-pounders. It was kindly loaned by the Rotunda Museum, and was taken up to Hartlepool in January 1983 for a fibre glass cast to be made of it.

As if that were not good fortune enough, later in 1983 the staff at Hartlepool heard of what was reported to be a 110-pdr. Armstrong breech loading gun of the 1860s on the island of Jersey, in the Channel Islands. Investigation revealed that the gun was guarding a statue (actually of General Sir George Don, lieutenant-governor of Jersey

Early Days at Hartlepool.

Concrete covers the upper deck.

PHOTOS: DAVE MORRELL

Time had taken its toll. Would anyone ever be able to restore this mess?

A 110 pdr breech loader.

from 1805-1814) in a public park in St Helier and, furthermore, that it was indeed an Armstrong breech-loader of *Warrior's* period.

It was mounted on a coast defence carriage, unlike those on board *Warrior,* but otherwise the gun was authentic, and in very good condition. The breech, which had been shut for years, opened, albeit stiffly, when it was tried. The muzzle had also been sealed for many years but when the plug was removed the rifling inside the barrel was in good condition. It was found to have 76 grooves, 0.06'' deep and 0.166'' wide, over a rifled length of 82½''. The 'twist' was about one-third of a turn in the length of the rifling. That gun was also kindly loaned by the Island of Jersey and in December 1983 it too was taken up to Hartlepool for a fibre glass replica to be made.

By September 1984, the upper deck had been completely planked and caulked, hatch coamings and skylights on the upper deck were completed, and the bulwarks with hammock nettings running along their tops were virtually finished. On 14 September, to celebrate this 'topping up', the Manifold Trust gave a buffet lunch party for the labour force and their wives.

Down below, less obtrusive but just as important work was being done, to clean and repaint the labyrinthine three-dimensional maze of *Warrior's* compartments. Some, like the engine room and boiler rooms, were vast and echoing as cathedrals. Others were so tiny a full-grown man could barely crawl inside. All had to have the accumulated debris of over a century removed and were then descaled with needle guns wielded by the 'Heavy Brigade' wearing ear muffs and heavy helmets with face guards. It took the 38-strong Brigade two years to finish the work. After scaling, all iron surfaces were coated with preservative before painting.

In some places, as many as 120 coats of paint had to be scaled off. 19th Century paint contained a much higher percentage of lead than would be permissible in modern paints. Stringent safety precautions had to be taken whilst removing it, exactly as though it were radio-active. The workmen wore special face-masks and clothing, worked in specially cordoned-off areas, and had to be decontaminated every time they left the ship.

Nevertheless, in September 1984, in spite of all the work that had already been done, above and below, and all the

Headquarters for the Restoration Project. The old Custom House at Hartlepool just 100 yds from the ship.

allowances that could be made for *Warrior's* appearance, she still looked—not to be mealy-mouthed about it—basically a hulk. But on 25th of that month, the mizzen mast was stepped. At once, *Warrior* took on the appearance of a proper ship. From that day on, even the doubters and 'Disgusted of Hartlepool' in the local paper were convinced that *Warrior* was really going to be restored.

The mizzen is the aftermost and smallest of *Warrior's* masts but its statistics are still impressive. The lower mast is 84 feet long from its base on the lower deck in the centre of the wardroom to its top. The top mast is 50 feet long, with a mean diameter of 16 inches. The topgallant and royal masts, made in one section, are another 40 feet. The distance from the top or truck of the mast down to the upper deck is 153 feet. The mizzen top, the wooden platform where the lower and top masts overlap, is 10½ feet by 20 feet, and has strengthening bands of steel.

Warrior's original masts were made of wood, replaced by iron in the 1870's, but the modern masts are made of steel (some of them surplus from oil rigs). The lower mizzen mast, 26 inches in diameter and weighing 13 tons, was hoisted by a specially-hired giant crane. Although it appeared simple and all went smoothly to a layman's eye, it was in fact a complicated and very delicate operation.

The mast had to be accurately lowered through holes cut in the upper and main decks with very tight clearances of between an eighth and a quarter of an inch. The holes were cut so that the mast had a rake of 4½ degrees towards the stern.

The mizzen topmast had been tested in position whilst it and the lower mast were lying horizontally on the quay, then slid back and lashed alongside the lower mast. To save crane hire expense, the lower and top masts were hoisted on board in one move. The topmast was later hoisted upwards into its proper position through the mizzen maintop, just as it was done in 1861.

Only two months later, on 19 November 1984, the much longer and heavier main mast, the largest of the three, was stepped. The lower mainmast was 120 feet long, had a diameter of 3 feet 6 ins, and with the main top mast weighed 33 tons. It was lowered through the upper, main and lower decks, to be stepped, with a rake of 3½ degrees towards the stern, on the orlop deck double bottom girder between the cable lockers.

On 6 February 1985, there was the most dramatic symbol yet of the progress being made when the great figurehead, the armoured Roman warrior with his feathered helmet and his shield (but without his more vulnerable sword,

September 1985. Temporary buildings and workshops have sprung up around the ship—and the new masts are going up too . . .

which was kept until nearer the day of completion) was hoisted over the bows and slotted onto the beak. The original figurehead was actually preserved ashore until comparatively recently, but was destroyed in the 1970s. The new figurehead was made out of 3 tons of yellow pine, assembled and glued, ready for carving by two craftsmen on the Isle of Wight, Jack Whitehead and Norman Gaches.

The appearance of this striking figurehead on the stand provided by the *Daily Express* at the 1983 Boat Show, and subsequently on the 'Blue Peter' TV programme, brought *Warrior* and her restoration some priceless publicity. The figurehead was then placed outside the 'Mary Rose' shop in Portsmouth, where it drew further attention, as an earnest that one day *Warrior* would return to Portsmouth.

On 20 February 1985, the foremast was stepped in the morning, and the bowsprit in the afternoon. The appearance of the bowsprit, that great spar jutting out emphatically towards the main road, brought passing traffic to a halt and cameras out of glove compartments. It was perhaps the most potent tourist attraction the town of Hartlepool had ever had.

The number of people employed on *Warrior's* restoration has risen dramatically since the early days of September 1979 when there were only four employees. A year later there were seventeen. By 1983 there were 34 permanent

full-time personnel and another 38 from the Manpower Services Commission. By the beginning of 1985 the *Warrior* work force was approaching its peak of 150 people, about half of them from the Manpower Services Commission.

Those who came through the Manpower Services Commission usually left when their year was up—although at least one of them, Lorraine Bird, stayed on as Walter Brownlee's assistant historian and keeper of records. The great majority of the permanent employees were time-served tradesmen, who had served full apprenticeships as draughtsmen, welders, fitters, riggers, caulkers, electricians, platers, painters, drillers, burners, boiler-makers and shipwrights.

These skilled men had previously worked for ship-building firms throughout the north-east. Those firms had cut their work forces, or disappeared altogether—and so too, the redundant men had thought, had the need for their skills. They were therefore delighted and privileged to work again on a ship, especially a ship who as they say themselves 'has a bit of class about her', and to use again skills learned in their youth, which they had thought had gone for ever.

Under Tom Dulake, the Managing Director of the Warrior Preservation Trust, who 'joined' *Warrior* in December 1979, are Bill Stevenson, time-served shipyard draughtsman with Sir William Gray's Yard, who joined *Warrior* in October 1980 and became project manager in September 1983 when Ray Hockey had to leave because of illness; Stan Morrell, ship manager, time-served shipwright with S.P. Austin & Son Ltd, who joined in October 1979; Keith Johnson, draughtsman supervisor, time-served draughtsman with Swan Hunter, who joined in November 1980; Jim Wilson, project engineer, who served his time with Central Marine Engine Works, went to sea with Ellerman City Line and Clan Line, and joined *Warrior* in November 1984; Mrs Jean Bartram, who joined on 3 September 1979, as personal assistant and secretary to the directors; and Mrs Joan Docherty, cleaner/tea lady/general factotum, who joined in November 1980.

From the early days in 1979, and throughout the restoration, the Trust has obtained the advice, on a consultancy basis, of Ron Clark, C. Eng., F.R.I.N.A., managing director of Burness Corlett & Partners (W.H.) Ltd, Basingstoke, naval architects and maritime transport consultants.

In the two years since the spring of 1985 the restoration work made tremendous strides. Even after an absence of only a week a visitor could see some differences—something added, or erected or newly decorated. All three masts were completed with standing rigging, with gaffs, and crossed with lower, topsail and topgallant yards. The bowsprit was extended to the 1862 length, with jib and boom and flying jibboom. Steel wire was used instead of the original iron wire and polypropylene nylon rope instead of the old tarred Italian hemp. Duralon canvas sails were furled on the yards: it was found that best way to simulate a furled sail was to make a real sail and furl it.

The ornate carving on the beak, the entry port and the stern gallery, was restored by Richard Barnett, a craftsman from Devon. The upper deck itself was completed, and provided with all the gear and impedimenta for working the sails—the fife rails, bitts and tackles; the bow and stern 110-pdr Armstrong guns, on revolving carriages so that they could fire on each bow and quarter, and astern; the secondary armament of four 40 pounders; the two flying bridges; the ship's boats; the two funnels, hydraulically retractable; the ventilators; the steering wheels; the rifle tower; anchors at bow and stern; the hatchways and skylights; and the hammock nettings along the bulwarks.

On the main deck, every gun was placed in position at its gunport, complete with gear and tackle for training, elevating, firing, clearing and reloading. Every mess was given its table, benches, utensils and crockery. On both sides of the main deck, the anchor cables were laid out, running from forward to the cable lockers, with their compressors, amidships.

All the features of the maindeck, as familiar now to those who had worked on them as though they had actually served in the ship, were completed and installed: the main galley stove, the two capstans, the four steering

JUST TWO OF "THE TEAM"

Keith Johnson—Supervisor of the draughtsmen.

Jean Bartram—Secretary and PA to the Directors kept the paperwork flowing.

wheels, the main engine room hatch, the messenger rollers, the Downton pumps with their handles in their stowages, the coal-holes in the deck itself and the scuttles for handing up ammunition. Round solid shot was stowed in racks and there were more racks full of Enfield rifles, Colt revolvers and cutlasses. Aft, the Captain's day cabin and sleeping quarters, and the Commander's and Master's cabins, were all furnished.

On the lower deck, wardroom, gunroom and officers cabins were repainted and redecorated to an appearance

THE SHIP COMES TO LIFE . . .

Compare this photograph to the one on page 48?

The main galley range.

October 1986—Restoration is nearly complete. Every detail is checked and double checked.

Plenty of muscle power was needed to steer the ship in the days before hydraulics—hence 4 wheels.

The Launderette! An early washing machine onboard.

probably a great deal smarter than anything Jackie Fisher and Midshipman Murray would have recognised. Forward, on the freshly white painted flats, the bag racks, issue room, slop room, cells, sick bay dispensary, store rooms and sail room have all been restored, and below them the ship's company drying room, the magazines, the propellor shaft tunnel, and the machinery spaces.

The aim has been to restore *Warrior* as nearly as possible to the way she was in her first commission, from 1861 to 1864. But what exactly did she look like? To find that out has been the principal task over the years of Walter Brownlee, assisted by Lorraine Bird and *Warrior's* London-based researcher, Antonia MacArthur, who have pursued the goals of accuracy and authenticity with a determination amounting almost to obsession.

Many of the best clues were to be found in the ship herself. She at least was authentic. In this sense the restoration was like an archaeological dig. Just as archaeologists examine pottery shards, bones, coins and other artefacts, so *Warrior's* restorers had to assess the significance of a compartment's construction or dimensions, the possible uses of a bulkhead clip, or the meaning of a series of drilled holes—always bearing in mind that the Victorians were shrewd and ingenious engineers and ship-builders and did nothing without a good reason.

The restorers had also to decide which fittings had been added later and were superfluous or irrelevant. It was, as Walter Brownlee says, like detective work—covering hundreds of items, over more than a hundred years.

The Public Record Office at Kew has Admiralty documents in profusion, dealing with every aspect of *Warrior's* design, construction and service history. Many of the original ship builders' drawings are still in existence. But they had to be treated with care. Victorian ship's drawings often showed items as designed or as intended-not 'as fitted'. There often were crucial changes between drawing board and ship.

Much contemporary information still exists. There are ship-builders' models of *Warrior* in the Science Museum in South Kensington, and a series of models of ships' fittings and equipment, some of them relevant to *Warrior,* which were made for the Paris Exhibition in 1861 and are still preserved in the National Maritime Museum.

There are contemporary illustrations, such as drawings in the *Illustrated London News.* But these too had to be treated with reserve. It was not unknown for an artist to take artistic licence and draw diminished human figures so as to exaggerate the scale of the ship-building achievement. There are also some contemporary photographs, few but excellent, showing the ship's external appearance and some scenes on deck. From one of these, for example, the size of the ship's quadruple steering wheels was calculated, and the precise shape of the spokes—was obtained.

There are contemporary Admiralty instruction manuals, as well as books written by serving or retired naval and army officers, which give much information on ship handling, seamanship, guns, ammunition, gun drill and guns'

crews. *Nare's Seamanship* of 1862, for example, revealed that whereas nearly all rope used in the 19th Century Navy was 'right-hand lay', i.e. twisted clockwise, rope used in gun tackles was 'left hand lay'. The reason given was that left hand laid rope, made of the usual right-hand spun yarn, was less liable to part under the strain of gun recoils.

The problem with many contemporary sources is that they assume knowledge not possessed by the modern restorer. They often state that things should be done 'as usual in Her Majesty's Service', or 'to be fitted as directed'. *Warrior,* for example, was to be rigged 'as for an 80-gun ship'—one was expected to know how such a ship was rigged.

It was therefore with great joy and relief that the restoration team at Hartlepool made the acquaintance of Midshipman Murray, who did not asume that they already knew everything, indeed if anything he seemed to believe that everybody was as ignorant as he was himself. Midshipman Murray's journal, with its detailed drawings of the ship, was preserved in the Royal Naval Museum, Portsmouth, who kindly loaned the plans to the *Warrior* Preservation Trust.

Murray had a young man's inquisitive eye and a passion for detail. He noted where everything was, on each deck. In time 'what does Midshipman Murray say?' came to be one of the watchwords of the Restoration. His plans solved many queries and corrected not a few errors. For example, it showed that, contrary to previous belief, both the Commander and the Master had to share their cabins with a 68-pdr gun.

Certainly Murray's plans must have impressed his Captain, for a copy of them, similar except for minor details, was amongst a collection of Captain Cochrane's possessions which his descendants in Northern Ireland made available to *Warrior* and the Naval Museum. They included his full dress uniforms, boat cloaks and sword belts; his sextant and chart instruments; his dressing cases, and a large collection of silverware.

Also amongst this Cochranalia was another priceless contemporary source—the Captain's letter book, with longhand copies of every letter written by Captain Cochrane during the commission. There are some hundreds of letters dealing with every aspect of life on board: leave, food, advancements, punishments, stores, defects. Many of the letters concern the ship's structure, guns, and performance at sea, and cover a wide range of subject, from paint to diving dress, from barometers to steering gear, from 'flash' communications (an early form of signalling lamp) to gas lighting, from easy chairs in the after cabin to scaling ladders, from a new carpet for the Captain's cabin to a report on the Drying room.

In their discussions on how things must have been made or how they must have looked, Walter Brownlee, Stan Morrell, Keith Johnson and the others would act as 'devil's advocates'—when one made a suggestion, the others would say 'Prove it'. But when at last a solution did appear, many of the resulting ship's fittings and items of

AUTHORS PHOTO

The Boiler Room is nearly complete October 1986.

equipment were designed and made at Hartlepool by the restoration work force. Keith Johnson (who incidentally first spotted the 68 pounder barrel at Woolwich) and his drawing office team at the Custom House base, near the ship, produced more than 500 drawings—80 of them for the rigging alone.

Sometimes the restoration required great ingenuity as well as technical expertise. Jim Wilson and his project engineering team designed and built a complete replica of the Penn Horizontal Trunk Expansion engine. The engine itself stands 13 feet 3 inches high and its crankshaft is 30 feet long. There are two 112 inch diameter cylinders on the port side and a jet condenser on the starboard side.

The main steam pipe from the boiler room, 24 inches in diameter, is led from forward along the port side of the centre line into the engine room and thence to the valve chest and the pistons. The two pistons are attached via connecting rods to the crankshaft and move within open-ended trunks 41 inches in diameter.

Exhaust steam from the cylinders was piped over the crankshaft to the condenser, where it was cooled by a sea-water spray. Some of this condensate was fed back to the boilers, and the surplus water was pumped overboard. The basic engine structure was cast iron, with brass valves and bushes, and copper pipes.

Because of limitations of access within the ship, this giant replica engine, with all its pipes and cranks and trunks, had to be made so that every part of it was small enough to pass through an aperture only 8 feet by four. The engine was then erected *in situ*. For the benefit of visitors, the engine will actually be turned on board by an electric motor.

The cupola furnace for filling shells with molten iron is three-dimensional and life size. But the boilers are like a Hollywood film set. In front are the furnace doors and boiler fronts, reproduced in realistic materials and detail; behind, they are supported by staging. But two GWR trucks are still there.

The restoration work has provided much employment in Hartlepool. Local firms, mostly small engineering companies, manufactured many major items. E & F Fibre Glass cast the gun barrels, to an eerily lifelike metallic finish. Sandgate Precision Engineering made the 110-pdr carriage fittings, and IWS made the bower anchors. HQ Engineering made the boat davits, machined the 30 foot crank shaft and the main bearings, fabricated the main propellor—only one blade was necessary, because visitors will see only the tip of it—and manufactured items such as the elevating screws for the Armstrong 110-pounders.

Kellett Engineering made the plastic shells for the 68-pdr guns, and turned the capstan spindles. Specialist Welding & Fabrication made the galley stove, the Downton pumps,

The boilers . . . imagine the heat, dust and pitching movement in a heavy sea.

Mess Utensils. The whole of the restoration project aimed to give the visitor a view of the ship as she was in 1860—ten minutes after the crew had left.

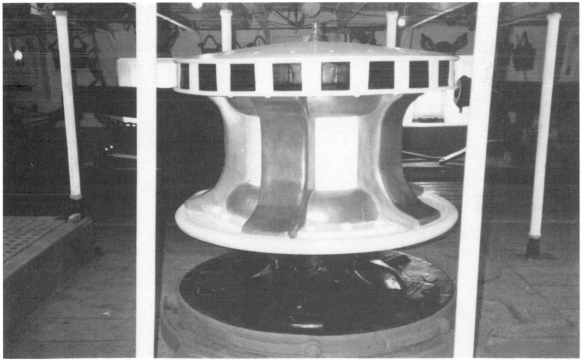

The Capstan.

the Victorian 'Tumbling' washing machine and the main deck messenger gear. Marble and Stone Craft made firebricks for the galley stove and the cupola furnace.

Not only local firms but local Colleges and Industrial Training Boards also contributed. Hartlepool College of Further Education, whose Principal Mr Colin Doram also happened then to be Chairman of the 'Friends of the Warrior', used the ship as a practical Special Skills project in their Engineering Industrial Training Board (EITB) Course. The 16-17 year old students reproduced replica gun tackle eyes, train tackle places, battledores and skylight hinges and, as their ultimate achievement, the massive crosshead tiller yoke of the steering gear.

Some of these gifts in kind saved the Trust considerable sums of money. To give just a small selection from a host of contributors: Sheffield EITB made hatch corner stanchion sockets and sets of bolts and rivet heads for 68-pdr carriages, for an estimated saving of £800. Gateshead Technical College made nine screw-well ventilators, to save £900. Billingham EITB made parts of four armoured citadel doors and three sets of fighting top stanchions, worth £1,300, as well as fabricating the two Rodger's stern anchors.

The North Eastern Training Association made the fore top mast, the main and fore topsail yards, and the painter's punt—all together worth £17,000. The South West Durham EITB made one upper yoke, the main topmast, three wheel indicators and some 100-pdr elevating screws, to save nearly £10,000. Cleveland Council of Churches CP Scheme provided a variety of items, including 68-pdr cannon balls, 110-pdr shot, lanyard toggles, quoin handles, rammers and sponges, pistol ready racks, fire bucket stands, and foundry and marine shop patterns, for a total value of well over £5,000.

The work was by no means done entirely in the northeast. The Royal Ordnance Factory at Birtly made 20 sets of 68-pdr sights and a set of 110-pdr sights, worth £4,400. The Royal Ordnance Factory at Nottingham refurbished one 40-pdr gun and made one carriage, saving the Trust £5,000. Messrs Wood Bros. (Drayton) Ltd of Portsmouth made and presented 30 sailors' ditty boxes. The ship's bell, hanging just forward of the main mast on the main deck, was found at the Naval Ordnance Museum in Gosport by Captain John Wells and presented to *Warrior* by the Museum. The decorative bell-rope was made and presented by Chief Petty Officer George Mercer of Portsmouth.

Over the years, the work of bringing *Warrior* to life has been recorded more closely and intimately than almost any other work of restoration, using video tapes, photographs and slides. At least one roll of 36-exposure film has been expended every working day for several years. Although the exterior looks authentically Victorian, hidden from sight behind panelling are miles of wires and cables for lighting, fire alarm systems, video recorders, and closed circuit TV. *Warrior* may be a Victorian ship but she had to conform to modern fire precaution standards; to observe these, an extra, decidedly non-Victorian, non-

AUTHORS PHOTO

authentic (and, to some, heretical) gangway has had to be cut in an originally unbreached main transverse bulkhead.

Many firms and organisations have made donations, amongst them (again, the list is anything but exhaustive) the National Memorial Heritage Fund, English Heritage, BICC, Kleinwort Merchant Bankers, Humphrey Whitbread, the Science Museum, South Kensington, and the English Tourist Board. The Manpower Services Commission was a major source of finance—£300,000 in 1985 and £400,000 in 1986—and will have contributed well over £1 million by the time *Warrior* leaves Hartlepool.

There have also been contributions from donations, deeds of covenant, admission charges and sales of souvenirs, amounting nearly to £½ million. But even such sums as these are still far short of the total required, which by 1986 was already over £5 million and may well rise above £6 million. The balance, of nearly £4 million, has been provided by the extraordinary generosity of the Manifold Trust. The money has been raised by John Smith, from his office in Dean's Yard, Westminster. As he says himself, 'I just sit there at the desk and make it'.

Warrior research concerned people as well as objects. Great efforts were made to trace "Old *Warriors*"—defined as those who had served in HMS *Warrior* (1860) up to 1924 when she was *Vernon III*; direct descendants of those who had served in HMS *Warrior* (1860); those who had served in the light fleet carrier *Warrior* between 1944 and 1971.

Anchors of all shapes and sizes are prepared.

There were several in the first category, including Chief Petty Officer Telegraphist Charles Cutler, aged 98, who served in *Vernon III* in 1908; Mr Sam Waller, aged 86, who was an electrical artificer under training in *Vernon III* in 1918; and Mr Arthur Ferret, aged 90, who qualified as a Seaman Torpedoman on board in 1916. At the Southsea RNLI Fair in 1983, Mr L.V. Little, aged 82, came up to the *Warrior* stand and announced himself as having served in *Vernon III* as a Boy Seaman in 1920.

There was also a surprising number of "Old *Warriors*" in the second category, including several who were descendants of men who had served in *Warrior's* first commission. Among them are Lieutenant Michael Cochrane, RN, great grand nephew of Captain Cochrane; Mr C.W.M. Kerry, great grand nephew of Chief Engineer William Glasspole (1861—1864); Mr David Rawlings, great grandson of Ord. Seaman James Webber (1861-64); Mrs Meehan, granddaughter of Gunner C. Houghton RM (1862—64); Mrs Irene Millest, granddaughter of William Mallion, Gunner RMA (1861—1864); Mrs E.P. Moyes great granddaughter of Gunner Robert Hill RMA, (1861—1863); Commander R.A.C. Owen RN, grandnephew of Lieutenant Hastings Owen RN, (1861—1863); Mr Robert Selby, grandson of Midshipman and later Lieutenant Walter Hailstone (1861, and 1881—82); Mrs Alex Stanley, great niece of Master George Henry Blakey, (1861—1864); Mrs L.S. Gillingham and Mr D. Houghton, great great great grandchildren of Chief Engineer William Buchan (1861—67); and Mr Keith Kissack, grandson of Harry A. Keith Murray, Midshipman (1861—1863) and Lieutenant (1870—1871).

THE FINAL JOURNEY . . .

*Almost ready to move. Warrior **spends her last winter at Hartlepool whilst the final preparations are made for her journey south.***

Warrior left Hartlepool on 12 June 1987, under the charge of tugs of the Alexandra Towing Co. the same company whose tugs had brought her from Milford Haven all those years before. It was a bitterly cold day, with pouring rain, but thousands of people and several bands turned up to say their farewells and wish 'God speed to the *Warrior*'. Outside, she was met and escorted for some way by a modern warship, the frigate HMS *Arrow*. There were many wet eyes and lumps in throats—and a huge aching gap alongside the Old Coal Dock—when she was gone.

Portsmouth was *Warrior's* destination. The City Council had made no secret of their delight at the prospect of having her. *Warrior* would take her place in the Naval Heritage Area, at the southern end of the dockyard, along with Nelson's *Victory* and Henry VIII's *Mary Rose*.

The 390 mile tow down to Portsmouth took place without incident, in smooth seas and calm weather. The passage had been planned so that *Warrior* passed through the Straits of Dover in daylight. But she was well ahead of schedule, was off Shoreham at 8.00 am on Monday morning, 15 June, and next day arrived in the Solent where she exchanged identities with HMS *London*. Thus the Navy's oldest battleship met the Navy's newest warship, a Type 22 frigate. *Warrior* spent much of the day standing off in the Solent, waiting for the afternoon

tide—and for her grand entrance.

Warrior's arrival in Portsmouth Harbour on 16 June 1987 was an occasion which surpassed any of her Victorian glories. She was met by over ninety boats, with helicopters overhead, water cannon and fireworks. The shore was black with people, thousands and thousands, lining Southsea Common, the Hot Walls and the Camber to welcome her.

Waiting for *Warrior* was her new berth, just inside the Victory Gate and within plain view of The Hard, Portsmouth Harbour Station and the Isle of Wight ferries. It had been specially designed for her by the Director of Engineering for Portsmouth City and built by W.A. Dawson Ltd of Luton, at an estimated cost of about £1½ million.

The Lord Mayor of Portsmouth, Councillor John Marshall, officially inaugurated the start of dredging operations on 1 March 1985. The berth was dredged to a depth of 8 metres by a sub-contractor, Zanen Dredging and Construction Ltd. A work force of 20 men on board the 400 ton dredger *Loch Reach* worked 12 hours a day, seven days a week, to remove 56,000 cubit metres of soft clay, the silt being dumped near the Nab Tower.

The dredging was obstructed by the foundations of the old Victorian railway viaduct which originally ran from the

Farewell Hartlepool . . . One of the Royal Navy's more modern frigates—HMS Arrow—sails past Warrior as she sets out on her voyage south. Although not welcomed by all when she arrived in Hartlepool she was sorely missed when she sailed . . .

C IN C FLEET

FOTOFLITE

Photographed in the Dover straights as she heads for Portsmouth.

Harbour Station to South Railway Jetty in the dockyard. As always, the Victorian engineers built to last. The foundations were cast iron tubes with spiral bits like drills at their lower ends. They had been literally screwed down into the soft harbour bed until they met a hard substrata. They resisted all attempts to dislodge them and had eventually to be broken off below seabed level. About 400 timber pile stumps had also to be dredged up from the harbour.

The Jetty is 590 feet long by 23 feet wide, and its construction involved driving in 93 steel piles, precasting 22 concrete cross beams and 42 end beams, fabricating 260 deck beams and positioning 1,000 cubic metres of concrete. It has two specially designed access gangways.

Bollards were originally provided on the jetty but these were only necessary for *Warrior's* initial berthing. At first, the ship was berthed alongside catamarans. Ten days were then spent in the delicate process of hauling on wires and chains with specially fitted hydraulic winches, lining up the ship to leading marks ashore, and the catamarans were removed. *Warrior* is now 'resiliently moored', so that she remains permanently some eight to ten feet off the jetty. She is kept in her correct position against tides and winds by an 'eight leg' mooring system, devised by marine consultants Captain Colin McMullen and Associates, using ground chains and anchors, laid in dredged trenches, with concrete sinkers.

The last lap. As she approaches Portsmouth Naval Base the spectator boats arrive to escort her for the last couple of miles.

Home at last. Back in Portsmouth—the port from which she was towed on March 13, 1929—as a hulk.

Also waiting to meet *Warrior* was her new commanding officer, Captain Colin Allen RN, wearing specially-grown sideboards of Victorian luxuriance, a naval cap of Victorian pattern and a uniform frock coat specially cut and made for him by the 'Royal cutter', Mr Jones, and Gieves & Hawkes—Mr Robert Gieve having taken a very close interest in the *Warrior* restoration project. Captain Allen was 'headhunted' for his new command by the Warrior Preservation trust. In fact, one of his final appointments in the Navy had been Chief Staff Officer (Administration) on the staff of Flag Officer Portsmouth, where he was himself much involved in the arrangements and preparations for *Warrior's* arrival and berthing in Portsmouth.

Amongst the waiting crowds was Jean Bartram, who had watched *Warrior* being towed into Hartlepool in 1979. 'In those days everybody said she was nothing better than a hulk. But even then you could see what a lovely ship she was, what a graceful shape, and what she could become one day'. Having said farewell at Hartlepool, Jean Bartram and her husband drove down to welcome *Warrior* to Portsmouth. 'She was the most wonderful, exhilarating sight. The TV pictures didn't begin to do justice to her'. With that, *Warrior's* story may be said to have come round full circle.

W. SARTORI

New Era—New Captain. Captain Colin Allen—In the correct "rig of the day".

Warrior at her new home— ready to be seen by a new generation.

W. SARTORI

Principal Dates in *Warrior's* History

1859

29 April: Tenders called for.

11 May: Order placed with Thames Ironworks.

25 May: First keel plate laid.

John Penn & Sons' tender for engine, boilers and propellor hoisting gear accepted.

5 October: named *Warrior*.

1860

29 December: Launch.

1861

1 August: First Commissioned.

17 October: Official Speed trials in Stokes Bay.

24 October: Accepted into service.

31 October: Sailed on first cruise, to Ireland.

1862

21 January: Sailed for cruise to Lisbon and Gibraltar.

March to June: Devonport for Alterations.

1863

2—7 March: escorted Princess Alexandra, Flushing to Gravesend.

March to June: Devonport for refit and alterations.

11 July: To sea with Channel Squadron for Round Britain Cruise.

1 October: Plymouth Sound after cruise.

15 December: Sailed for cruise to Madeira, Teneriffe, Gibraltar, Lisbon.

1864

5 March: Arrived Portland after cruise.

22 November: Paid off at Portsmouth into 2nd Division of the Reserve for first major refit lasting 2½ years, during which ship was re-armed.

1867

1 July: Commissioned with complement of *Black Prince* for service as flagship at Queenstown.

17 July: Took part in Spithead Review for Sultan of Turkey and the Khedive of Egypt.

24 July: Paid off (Queenstown appointment cancelled).

25 July: Recommissioned at Spithead.

25 October: Sailed for cruise along Portuguese coast.

28 December: At anchor in Cowes Roads.

1868

1 January to 22 February: At Cowes rowing daily guards off Queen Victoria's residence at Osborne because of Fenian activity.

12—25 April: Escorted Royal Yacht *Victoria & Albert* from Holyhead to Dublin and back.

14 August: Collision with *Royal Oak*.

17 December: Sailed for Lisbon.

1869

7 May: Returned after cruises of Portuguese coast.

17 June: Sailed for Madeira, joined by *Black Prince* at sea.

4 July: Started towing Floating Dock to Bermuda.

29 July: Arrived off Bermuda.

25 August: Anchored Spithead.

19 October: Sailed for extended cruises to Lisbon, Madeira, Teneriffe, Gibraltar, Vigo, Corunna, the Azores.

1870

6 June: Anchored Spithead (after longest period ever away from UK).

4 August: Weighed for Gibraltar.

August and September: Channel Squadron cruises with Mediterranean Fleet.

6/7 September: *Captain* capsized and sank.

1871

30 April: Sailed from Plymouth Sound to Bantry Bay, Madeira, Gibraltar.

1 July: *Agincourt* aground on Pearl Rock.

6 August: Sailed to join fleet of 23 major British warships from Channel Squadron, Mediterranean Fleet, Flying Squadron and 1st Reserve Squadron.

15 September: Paid off at Portsmouth. End of service as first line warship.

Second major refit.

1875

1 April: Commissioned as seagoing ship of 1st Reserve stationed at Portland.

29 July: Sailed Portland for round-Ireland cruise.

1 September: *Vanguard* rammed and sunk by *Iron Duke* off Kish Light.

1876

At Portland: quarterly firings, spring docking, annual inspection, summer cruise to Gibraltar to reinforce Channel Squadron because of tension with Russia.

1877

At Portland: Summer cruise to Vigo and Arosa.

1878

3 July: Sailed Portland with Reserve Particular Service Squadron, formed because of further tension with Russia.

13 August: Queen Victoria reviewed Particular Service squadron at Spithead before it dispersed at the end of Russian crisis.

1879

At Portland.

1880
29 June: Hit Portland breakwater.

1881
At Portland.
15 June: Sailed with Reserve Squadron for cruise to Heligoland, Kiel and Cronstadt.
27 September: To sea for new station at Greenock.

1882
At Greenock.

1883
8 May: Sailed for Portsmouth.
11 May: Anchored at Spithead. End of last sea-going passage not under tow.
31 May: Paid off for the last time as sea-going ship.

1902
16 July: Commissioned as Stationary Depot Ship for Destroyers and Torpedo Boats, flying pennant of Captain, Portsmouth Flotilla.

1904
31 March: Paid off.
1 April: Commissioned as Torpedo School Ship, HMS *Vernon*.

1923
Vernon became shore establishment.

1924
31 March: *Warrior* paid off as part of *Vernon*.

1927
22 October: Taken in hand for conversion to oil fuel pontoon hulk.

1929
March: Towed Pembroke Dock, South Wales.

1942
27 August: Redesignated 'Oil Fuel Hulk C.77'.

1979
Scheduled for scrapping.
Taken over by Maritime Trust for restoration.
August/September: Towed Hartlepool.

1987
12 June: Left Hartlepool under tow after restoration.
16 June: Arrived Portsmouth.
27 July: Open to visitors at Portsmouth.

Open to the public at last 27 July 1987.

W. SARTORI

84

Warrior's Senior Officers

Flag Officers

26 July—9 September 1875: Vice Admiral Sir John Walter Tarleton (during cruise in which *Vanguard* was rammed and sunk by *Iron Duke*).

5 June—16 August 1878: Rear Admiral Henry Boys, as flag Officer Second in Command of Particular Service Squadron formed during the Russian 'scare' mobilisation.

Captains

1 August 1861—22 November 1864 (paid off for long refit): The Hon Arthur Cochrane.

1—24 July 1867: John Corbett (commission prematurely ended).

25 July 1867—20 August 1869: Henry Boys (who later flew his flag in *Warrior*).

21 August 1869—21 February 1870: Frederick A. Stirling.

22 February 1870—15 September 1871 (paid off for long refit): The Hon. Henry C. Glyn.

1 April 1875—14 March 1878: William H. Whyte.

15 March 1878—29 April 1881: R. Gordon Douglas.

30 April 1881—26 November 1882: Samuel P. Townsend.

27 November 1882—31 May 1883 (paid off from seagoing service): Edward S. Adeane.

16 July 1902—29 May 1905 (as stationary depot ship flying pennant of Captain Portsmouth Destroyer and Torpedo Boat Flotilla): John M. de Robeck.

30 May—29 August 1903: Arthur Dodgson.

30 August—31 December 1903: Seymour E. Erskine.

1 January—31 March 1904 (paid off and passed to *Vernon* as *Vernon III*): Edward F.B. Charlton.

Commanders

10 August 1861—9 September 1864: George Tryon (who was lost on 22 June 1893, as C-in-C Mediterranean, when his flagship *Victoria* was rammed and sunk by *Camperdown*, flagship of his second-in-command, Rear Admiral Markham, who also served as Commander in *Warrior*).

10 September—22 November 1864: William Codrington

3 August 1867—7 July 1870: Guy O. Twiss.

8 July 1870—15 September 1871: Alfred Markham.

1 April 1875—25 September 1877: William G. Scott.

26 September 1877—25 September 1879: Frank Rougemont.

26 September 1879—30 April 1881: Robert W. Davies.

1 May 1881—1 May 1882: Ernest M. Rolfe.

2 May 1882—31 May 1883: Charles E. Gissing.

No Commander borne during short commission of 1867, nor during 1902—04 period as Portsmouth depot ship.

10 February—31 May 1904: Harry L.D'E Skipwith.

Admiral of the Fleet Lord Fisher served in *Warrior* as Gunnery Lieutenant, aged 22, from 28 March 1863 until the end of March 1864.

HMS *Warrior's* Authorized Establishment, on Commissioning, 1 August 1861

Pay/Day

Officers

	s.	d.		s.	d.
Captain	20	0	Two Assistant Surgeons	10	9
Commander	16	6	Second Master	7	6
Five Lieutenants (Senior)	11	0	Two Assistant Paymasters	5	0
(Junior)	10	0			
Master	13	0	Clerk	4	0
Chaplain	8	10	Two Master's Assistants	4	0
Surgeon	18	0	Six Naval Cadets	0	11
Paymaster	26	0	Assistant Clerk	2	6
Naval Instructor	5	9			
Ten Mates (Sub. Lts.) &	3	8	(Mate)		
Midshipmen	1	9	(Mid.)		

Warrant Officers

	s.	d.		s.	d.
Gunner	6	7	Carpenter	6	7
Boatswain	6	7			

Chief Petty Officers

	s.	d.		s.	d.
Master at Arms	2	3	Chief Quarter Master	2	3
Chief Gunner's Mate	2	3	Chief Carpenter's Mate	2	3
Chief Boatswain's Mate	2	3	Seamen's Schoolmaster	2	0
Chief Captain of the			Ship's Steward	2	0
Forecastle	2	3	Ship's Cook	2	0

First Class Working Petty Officers

	s.	d.		s.	d.
Four Ship's Corporals	2	0	Two Captains of the Maintop	2	0
Two Gunner's Mates	2	0	Two Captains of the Foretop	2	0
Five Boatswain's Mates	2	0	Two Captains of the Afterguard	2	0
Captain's Coxswain	2	0	Captain of the Hold	2	0
Two Captains of the			Sailmaker	2	3
Forecastle	2	0	Ropemaker	2	3
Seven Quartermasters	2	0	Carpenter's Mate	2	3
Coxswain of the Launch	2	0	Caulker	2	3
Yeoman of Signals	2	0	Plumber	2	3
Leading Stokers (See Steam Dept.)			Blacksmith	2	3
			Armourer	2	3

Second Class Working Petty Officers

Coxwain of the Barge	1	10	Cooper	1	11
Coxswain of the Pinnace	1	10	Caulker's Mate	1	11
Two Captains of the Mast	1	10	Musician	1	11
Two Second Captains of the Forecastle	1	10	Twenty Leading Seamen	1	9
			Four Shipwrights	1	10
Four Second Captains of the Maintop	1	10	Three Yeomen of Store Rooms	1	8
			Two Second Captains of the Hold	1	8
Four Second Captains of the Foretop	1	10	Two Painters	1	8
			Three Sailmaker's Crew	1	8
Two Second Captains of the Afterguard	1	10	Two Blacksmith's Crew	1	8
			Two Armourer's Crew	1	8
Two Captains of the Mizentop	1	10	Eight Carpenter's Crew	1	8
Two Sailmaker's Mates	1	11	Cooper's Crew	1	8
Coxswain of the Cutter	1	10	Tinsmith	1	8
Two Signalmen	1	10			

Sixty-Four Able Seamen	1	7	Subordinate Officer's Cook	1	4
Three Sick Berth Attendants	1	6	Engineer's Servant	1	4
Twelve Bandsmen	1	4	Ship's Steward's Assistant	1	4
Two Tailors	1	4	Sixty-Four Ordinary Seamen	1	3
Two Butchers	1	4	Two Cook's Mates	1	1
Captain's Steward	1	4	Barber	1	1
Captains Cook	1	4	Sixty-Five Second Class Ordinary Seamen	1	0
Ward or Gun Room Steward	1	4			
Ward or Gun Room Cook	1	4	Ship's Steward's Boy	0	7
Commander's Servant	0	11	Twenty-Nine Boys First Class	0	7
Subordinate Officer's Steward	1	4	Twenty-Three Boys Second Class	0	6

Steam Department

Two Chief Engineers	12	3	Forty-Eight Stokers and Coal Trimmers	2	0
Nine Assistant Engineers	7	4			
Nine Leading Stokers	2	3	Eighteen Stokers 2nd Class	1	8

Marine Artillery

Captain	12	1	Three Bombardiers	2	0
Two Lieutenants	6	6	A Hundred and Fourteen Gunners	1	3¼
Three Sergeants	2	9¼	Two Drummers	1	5¼

Two ? Makers	1	4	Two Wardroom Servants	0	11
Lamp Trimmer	1	4	Ward Room Cook's Assistant	0	11
Engineers' Cook	1	4	Gun Room Servant	0	11
Captain's Servant	0	11	Gun Room Cook's Assistant	0	11
Captain's Cook's Assistant	0	11			

Daily Routines

Harbour Routine

A.M.   **SUMMER**

4.40 — Call boatswain's mates, corporals, and mates of decks.

4.45 — Hands.

4.50 — Hands fall in, scrub upper deck. Duty boats' crews clean out.

5.45 — Hammock stowers, royal yardsmen, and boys lash up and stow, royal yardmen clean conductors, spread awnings.

6.00 — Lash up and stow.

6.10 — Steerage hammock men, watch below fall in, sound reveille.

6.15 — Cooks, up guard and steerage hammocks, bathe.

6.30 — Breakfast.

7.00 — Forenoon watch to clean in blue working dress, duty men and boats' crews in rig of the day. Watch below clean main deck and flats.

7.15 — Watch and duty boats' crews fall in, clean bright work, if top-gallant masts are down overhaul top-gallant rigging.

7.50 — Upper yardmen fall in, up all wet deck clothes.

8.00 — Evolution, then quarters clean guns.

8.35 — Mondays and Wednesdays clean pump gear.

8.50 — Return rags.

8.55 — Disperse, hands to clean.

9.10 — Roll, sweepers.

9.20 — Quarters, prayers.

9.45 — Watch drill.

10.00 — Drills as ordered.

11.00 — Cooks, watch below, up spirits.

11.30 — Clear up decks.

12.00 — Dinner.

P.M.

1.25 — Roll, sweepers.

1.30 — Watch fall in.

3.00 — Watch drill.

3.50 — Upper yardmen fall in.

4.00 — Evolution, quarters.

4.15 — Cooks, shift into night clothing

4.30 — Supper.

5.00 — Both watches fall in, furl awnings coil up ropes.

5.30 — Bathe, up boats not required.

7.10 — Steerage hammock men fall in.

7.15 — Stand by guard and steerage hammocks.

7.30 — Stand by hammocks.

8.30 — Clear up main deck.

9.00 — Out pipes, rounds.

9.30 — Pipe down.

A.M.   **WINTER**

5.10 — Call boatswain's mates, corporals, and mates of decks.

5.15 — Lash up and stow.

5.30 — Cooks.

5.45 — Breakfast.

6.15 — Hands to clean in blue working rig.

6.25 — Both watches fall in, clean upper deck, upper yardmen clean lightning conductors, duty boats' crew clean out, up guard and steerage hammocks.

7.00 — Watch below clean main deck and flats, watch dry upper deck, coil down ropes.

7.15 — Overhaul top-gallant rigging if top gallant masts are down.

7.50 — Upper yardmen fall in.

A.M. *(contd.)*

8.00 — Evolution, then quarters, clean
     guns.

8.35 — Clean arms Tuesdays and Thursdays
     clean pump gear Mondays and Wednesdays.

8.50 — Return arms or rags.

8.55 — Hands to clean.

9.10 — Roll, sweepers.

9.15 — Quarters.

9.45 — Watch drill.

10.00 — Watch fall in, drills as ordered.

11.00 — Cooks, watch below, up spirits.

11.30 — Clear up decks.

12.00 — Dinner.

P.M.

1.15 — Roll, sweepers.

1.20 — Watch fall in.

3.00 — Watch drill.

3.50 — Upper yardmen fall in.

4.00 — Evolution, quarters, coil up ropes.

4.30 — Cooks.

4.45 — Supper.

TUESDAY AND THURSDAY

Routine for Small Arms.

A.M.

8.40 — Return rags.

8.45 — Hands to clean.

9.00 — Clean arms.

9.10 — Roll, sweepers.

9.15 — G. put belts on or return arms.

9.20 — Quarters.

FRIDAY

A quarter of an hour is to be given for cleaning guns, then pump gear. Clean guns after quarters.

Sundays

SUMMER

A.M.

5.30 — Lash up and stow.

5.45 — Cooks.

6.00 — Breakfast.

6.25 — Steerage hammock men fall in.
     Reveille.

6.30 — Up guard and steerage hammocks,
     hands to clean in blue working rig,
     duty men in rig of the day.

6.45 — Watch below clean main deck, watch
     fall in, clean upper deck as
     ordered, then wood and bright work
     duty boats' crews lower and clean
     out.

7.30 — Duty boats' crews to clean.

WINTER

A.M.

7.50 — Quarters, clean guns.

8.30 — Disperse, hands to clean.

8.50 — Roll, watch fall in, clear up
     decks for divisions.

9.30 — Divisions, divine service.

P.M.

3.50 — Roll, sweepers.

4.00 — Quarters.

4.15 — Cook's hands shift into night
     clothing.

4.30 — Supper.

5.00 — Coil up ropes. If awnings are to be
     spread lash up at 5.15, spread
     awning at 5.30, furl at 5.00pm.

Sea Routine

SUMMER

A.M.

3.30 — Coil up ropes.
4.00 — Scrub decks.
5.45 — Re-set sails, etc.
6.00 — Spread awnings, hammock stowers, royal yardmen and boys lash up.
6.15 — Lash up and stow, royal yardmen clean lightning conductors.
6.25 — Steerage hammock men fall in.
6.30 — Reveille, cooks, up guard and steerage hammocks.
6.45 — Breakfast.
7.15 — Watch below clean lower deck, watch clean in blue working dress, duty men in rig of the day.
7.30 — Watch fall in, stations, clean bright work.
8.00 — Quarters, clean guns.
8.30 — Clean pump gear on Mondays and Wednesdays.
8.40 — Return rags.
8.45 — Disperse, hands to clean.
8.55 — Roll, sweepers.
9.00 — Quarters, prayers.
9.30 — Watch drill.
9.45 — Drill as ordered.
11.30 — Clear up decks.
12.00 — Dinner.

P.M.

1.25 — Roll, sweepers.
1.30 — Watch fall in, drills as ordered.
3.00 — Watch drill.
3.45 — Clear up decks, watch below shift into night clothing.
4.00 — Cooks, shift into night clothing.
4.15 — Supper.
4.45 — Roll, both watches furl awnings.
5.00 — Quarters, evolution.
7.10 — Steerage hammock men fall in.
7.30 — Stand by hammocks.
8.30 — Rounds.

WINTER

A.M.

3.30 — Coil up ropes.
4.00 — Scrub decks.
6.00 — Hammock stowers, royal yardmen, and boys lash up.
6.15 — Lash up and stow.
6.25 — Steerage hammock men fall in.
6.30 — Reveille, cooks, up guard and steerage hammocks.
6.45 — Breakfast.
7.15 — Watch below clean lower deck, watch clean in blue working dress, duty men in rig of the day.
7.30 — Watch fall in, re-set sails, clean wood and bright work.
8.00 — Quarters, clean guns.
8.25 — Clean arms.
8.35 — Return rags.
8.40 — Disperse, hands to clean.
8.50 — Roll, sweepers.
9.00 — Quarters, prayers.
9.30 — Watch drill.
9.45 — Drills as ordered.
11.30 — Clear up decks.
12.00 — Dinner.

P.M.

1.15 — Roll, sweepers.
1.20 — Watch fall in, drills as ordered.
3.00 — Watch drill.
3.30 — Shift into night clothing.
3.50 — Roll, sweepers.
4.00 — Quarters, evolution, cooks, supper.
7.10 — Steerage hammock men fall in.
7.15 — Down guard and steering hammocks.
7.30 — Stand by hammocks.
8.30 — Rounds.

TUESDAY AND THURSDAY
Routine for Small Arms

A.M.

8.25 — Return rags.
8.30 — Hands to clean.
8.45 — Clean arms.
8.50 — G. put belts on or return arms.
8.55 — Roll, sweepers.
9.00 — Quarters.

FRIDAY
A quarter of an hour only to clean guns, then pump gear. Clean guns after.

Weekly Routine

MONDAY

Air bedding.
8.00 — Cross upper yards.
9.00 — Lash up or inspect bedding.
9.45 — General exercise aloft.
3.00 — Watch drill.
4.00 — Down royal yards, evening quarters wash clothes, alternate weeks scrub hammocks.

TUESDAY

5.30 — Lash up and stow.
5.45 — Up, scrub hammocks.
6.00 — Spread awnings.
8.00 — Cross royal yards.
9.45 — Watch drill.
4.00 — Down top-gallant masts, evening quarters.

WEDNESDAY

7.15 — Overhaul top-gallant rigging.
8.00 — Cross royal yards, loose sails.
9.45 — Watch drill.
11.15 — Furl sails.
4.00 — Down top-gallant masts, evening quarters.

THURSDAY

7.15 — Overhaul top-gallant rigging.
8.00 — Cross royal yards.
9.30 — Landing party.
10.15 — Marines.
11.15 — Furl sails.
4.00 — Down royal yards, evening quarters wash clothes.

FRIDAY

7.15 — Cross royal yards.
8.00 — Prepare for action.
9.45— General quarters.
11.15 — Cross royal yards, down upper yards.
P.M. — Scrub canvas gear, up yards etc.

SATURDAY

3.00 — Up, clean hammocks, alternate weeks.
4.00 — Mend furl of sails, evening quarters.

On Tuesdays in winter.
6.25 — Up, scrub hammocks.

Sources

ADM 1/5729, Armament of *Warrior*

ADM 1/5732, Armstrong Gun Instruction, December 1860

ADM 1/5743, Remarks on design of *Warrior*

ADM 1/6018, Models of General Fittings of Men-of-War, including *Warrior*, made for Paris Exhibition of 1867

ADM 3/268, Invitation to launch of *Warrior*

ADM 53/8097—8102A, Logs of first commission, Channel Squadron, 1 August 1861 to 22 November 1864

ADM 53/8849, Log of second commission, 1 to 24 July 1867

ADM 53/9847—9850, Logs of third commission, Channel Squadron, 25 July 1867 to 15 September 1871

ADM 53/11400—11403, Logs of fourth commission, First Reserve ship, Portland, 1 April 1875 to 30 April 1881 (53/11400 actually missing)

ADM 53/11840—1, Logs of fifth commission, First Reserve ship, Greenock, 1 May 1881 to 31 May 1883

ADM 53/31953, Log of sixth commission, Stationery Depot Ship for Destroyers and Torpedo Boats, flying pennant of Captain, Portsmouth Flotilla

ADM 87/57, *Warrior*, Correspondence from Controller

ADM 87/70—76, Documents on *Warrior*

'Amphibian', *Loss of HMS Captain, 6th September, 1870*, The Naval Review, Vol. XL, No.3 August 1952

Archibald, E.H.H., *The Metal Fighting Ship in the Royal Navy 1860—1970*, Blandford Press, 1971

Ballard, Admiral G.A., CB *British Battleships of 1870*, The Mariner's Mirror, articles on various dates, from Volume XV (1929) to XX (1934), esp. The *Warrior* and *Black Prince*, Volume XVI (1930), pp.168—186.
The Black Battlefleet, Nautical Publishing Co. Ltd., and the Society for Nautical Research, 1980
'Memoirs', Part Two: Midshipman, The Mariner's Mirror, Vol. LXII (1976)

Baxter, Colin F., *The Duke of Somerset and the Creation of the British Ironclad Navy, 1859—66*, The Mariner's Mirror, Vol. LXIII, No.3 August 1977

Baynham, Henry, *Before the Mast: Naval Ratings of the 19th Century*, Hutchinson, 1971

Brown, D.K., *The First Steam Battleships*, The Mariner's Mirror, Vol. 63, No.4, November 1977
Developing the Armour for HMS Warrior, Warship 40, October 1986

Brownlee, Walter, *Warrior The first modern battleship*, Cambridge University Press, 1985

Campbell, Lt. Charles, RN, *The Interior Economy of a Modern Man-of-War*, The Journal of the Royal United Service Institution, Vol. XXVII, No. CXIX, 1883

Cochrane, Alexander, *The Fighting Cochranes*, Quiller Press, 1983, Ch. 29, Admiral the Hon. Sir Arthur Auckland Leopold Pedro Cochrane

Cochrane, Captain The Hon. Arthur, R.N., Letter Book of HMS *Warrior's* Commission, 1861—64, in manuscript

Colomb, Vice Admiral P.H., *Memoirs of Admiral The Rt. Hon. Sir Astley Cooper Key*, Methuen & Co., 1898, Chs, XV and XVI

Conway's All The World's Fighting Ships 1860—1905, Conway Maritime Press, 1979

Cornhill Magazine, Vol. III Jan. 1861, 'Reform in the Navy'
Vol. VIII 1863, 'The Inner Life of a Man of War'

Douglas, General Sir Howard, Bart., GCB, GCMG, DCL, FRS, *A Treatise on Naval Gunnery*, Fifth Edition, Revised, John Murray, 1860

Egerton, Mrs Fred, *Admiral of the Fleet Sir Geoffrey Phipps Hornby GCB, A Biography*, William Blackwood & Sons, 1896, Ch. VIII, HMS *Edgar*, 1863—1865

Emmerson, George S., *John Scott Russell*, John Murray, 1977. Ch.7, 'The Iron Warship'

Fisher, Admiral of the Fleet Lord, *Memories*, Hodder & Stoughton, 1919, Ch. X: Apologia Pro Vita Sua

Fitzgerald, Admiral C.C., *The Life of Admiral Sir George Tryon, KCB*, Blackwood & Sons, 1897, Ch. IV

Hough, Richard, *First Sea Lord: An Authorised Biography of Admiral Lord Fisher*, Severn House, 1969, Ch.2: Prelude to Greatness

Instructions for the Exercise and Service of Great Guns etc. on board Her Majesty's Ships, also Small Arms, Field Pieces etc., Her Majesty's Stationery Office, 1865

Laird Clowes, Sir William, *The Royal Navy A History from the Earliest Times to the Present*, Sampson Low, Marston, 1903, Volume VII

Lambert, Andrew, *Battleships In Transition: The Creation of the Steam Battlefleet 1815—1860*, Conway Maritime Press, 1984
Warrior: Restoring the World's First Ironclad, Conway Maritime Press, 1987

Lewis, Michael, *The Navy In Transition 1814—1864 A Social History*, Hodder & Stoughton, 1965

Lyon, David, *Steam, Steel and Torpedoes: The Warship in the 19th Century*. (The Ship No.8), HMSO, 1980

Macdonald, John, *Return of the Warrior*, Telegraph Sunday Magazine, No. 504 June 22 1986

Majendie, Captain Vivian Dering, R.A., *Ammunition: A Descriptive Treatise*, Eyre & Spottiswoode, 1867

Moore, John, Research Notes on *Warrior*, in typescript, 1980

Naval and Military Gazette, January 5, August 10, September 28, October 19, November 2, and December 21, 1861

Noble, Sam, A.B., *'Tween Decks in the Seventies'*, Sampson Low, Marston, 1925

Osbon, G.A., *The First of the Ironclads: The Armoured Batteries of the 1850's*, The Mariner's Mirror, Vol. 50, No. 3, August 1964

Pakington, Sir John, D.N.B.

Parkes, Oscar, OBE, AINA, *British Battleships: Warrior 1860 to Vanguard 1950*, Seeley Services, 1957

Reed, E.J., *Our Iron Clad Ships*, John Murray, 1869

Rowbotham, Cdr. W.B., *The First British Seagoing Ironclad*, RUSI Journal, 1962, pp. 315—321

    The Loss of HMS Vanguard, 1875, The Naval Review, Vol. XXXIX, No. 4 November 1951

Slaymaker, E., *The Guns of HMS Warrior*, Warship 37, 38, 39, January, July, August 1986

The Gallant British Tar, or, The Visit of the Channel Fleet to Liverpool, 1863, printed by J & J. Gardner, Portsea, 1864

The Times, Monday December 31, 1860. *Launch of the Warrior*

Trotter, Wilfred Pym, *The Royal Navy in Old Photographs*, Dent, 1975

Wainwright, Martin, *Rebirth of the Ironclad*, Country Life, March 6, 1986

Walker, Admiral Sir Baldwyn Wake, D.N.B.

Warrior News, Issues 1—15

Watts, Anthony J., *Pictorial History of the Royal Navy. Volume One: 1816—1880*, Ian Allan, 1970

Wells, Captain John G., CBE, DSC RN, *HMS Warrior: Progress Reports*, in The Mariner's Mirror, No. 1: Vol. 70, No. 1, February 1984; No. 2: Vol. 71, No. 2, May 1985; No. 3: Vol. 72, No. 4, November 1986

    Warrior: the final preparations, Warship World, Vol. 1, No. 10, Spring 1987

    The Immortal Warrior: Britain's First and Last Battleship, Kenneth Masen, 1987

White, Colin, *The End of the Sailing Navy*, Kenneth Mason, 1981

    Victoria's Navy: The heyday of steam, Kenneth Mason, 1983

White, Walter, (Ed.), *A Sailor-Boy's Log-Book: From Portsmouth to the Peiho*, Chapman & Hall, 1862

Winton, John, *Hurrah for the Life of a Sailor!: Life on the lower-deck of the Victorian Navy*, Michael Joseph, 1977, Ch. 13 'Hoisting the ruddy old twiddler'

    HMS Warrior, The Naval Review, Vol. 69, No. 4, October 1981

Acknowledgements

The Author would like to record the assistance of the following in the compilation of this book. Their help was greatly appreciated.

Vice Admiral Sir Patrick Bayly, KBE, CB, DSC, Jean Bartram, Lorraine Bird, Captain Walter Brownlee, MRIN, MNI, Maldwin Drummond, DL, JP, Tom Dulake, the Friends of *Warrior*, the late Ray Hockey, Keith Johnson, the late John Moore, John Smith, Bill Stevenson, Captain John Wells, Jim Wilson

INDEX

Achilles, HMS 25, 41, 43, 55
Adalbert of Prussia, Prince 9
Agincourt, HMS 36, 39, 40, 43
Albert, Prince 3
Alexandra of Denmark, Princess 9
Alfred, Prince 9, 43, 44
Allen, Capt. C. 82
Arthur, Prince 9
Asslin, Asst. Surg. William J., ... 18
Audacious, HMS 43

Ballard, Admiral George 21, 25, 43
Barnett, Richard 66
Bartram, Mrs Jean 66, 82
Bayly, Admiral Sir Patrick 55
Belcher, Admiral Sir Edward 4
Belleisle, HMS 43
Bellerophon, HMS 39
Bermuda Dock 36
Bird, Lorraine 65, 70
Black Prince, HMS 4, 9, 10, 16, 36, 41, 43
Blakey, Master George H. 17, 18, 23
Boys, Capt. Henry, RN 36, 41
Bristol, HMS 39
Brownlee, Capt. Walter 55, 56, 65, 70
Buchan, Ch. Eng. William 18, 75
Burgoyne, Capt. Hugh, RN 40

Cadmus, HMS 41
Caledonia, HMS 39, 41
Camperdown, HMS 7
Captain, HMS 39
Channel Squadron 8, 9, 10, 12, 21, 36, 39, 41
Clark, Ron 66
Cleveland Council of Churches 74
Cochrane, Capt. The Hon Arthur, RN ... 6, 7, 8, 10, 17, 23,
                                               32, 70, 75
Cochrane, Lt. Michael, RN 75
Cochrane, Lord 6
Coleman, Asst. Surg. Edmund W. 18
Coles, Capt. Cowper, RN 39, 40
Columbine, tender 39
Corbett, Capt. John, RN 36
Couronne, French Ship 3
Cutler, CPO Charles 75

Dacres, R—A Sydney Colpoys 9, 15, 35
Defence, HMS 9, 41, 43
De Robeck, Capt. John, RN 46
De Vries, Paymstr. John, RN 18, 23
Digby, Lt. Noel S.F., RN 18
Docherty, Mrs Joan 66
Dog Watches 27
Don, General Sir George 59
Doram, Colin 74
Drills 25, 43

Drummond, Maldwin 55
Dulake, Tom 55, 66
Dupuy de Lôme 3

E & F Fibre Glass 71
Edgar, HMS 9, 11
Egypt, Khedive of 36
        Viceroy of 9
Emerald, HMS 10
Engineering Industrial Training Board 74
    Billingham 74
    Hartlepool 74
    Sheffield 74
    South West Durham 74
Erzherog Ferdinand Max 41
Everitt, Lt. Herbert, RN 18

Ferret, Arthur 75
Fisher, Lt. J.F., RN 7, 11, 12, 35, 70
Food 26
Friends of *Warrior* 59, 74

Gaches, Norman 64
Garibaldi, Giuseppe 12
Gateshead Technical College 74
Gazelle 9
Gillingham, Mrs L.S. 75
Glasspole, Ch. Eng. William 18, 75
Gloire, French Ship 3, 4
Great Eastern, ss 5
Grog 27

Hector, HMS 41, 43
Hercules, HMS 39, 40, 41, 44
Hesse, Prince and Princess of 9
Hockey, Ray 55
Hornby, Capt. G. Phipps 10
Houghton, Mr D. 75
H.Q. Engineering 71

Illustrious, HMS 22, 23
Immortalite, HMS 41
Inconstant, HMS 39, 41
Invincible, French Ship 3
Invincible, HMS 4, 41
Iron Duke, HMS 41
I.W.S. 71

Jackson, Rev. Robert 18
James, Mr 46
Johnson, Chief Gnrs. Mate Abraham 35
Johnson, Keith 66, 70, 71

94

What do you think of this book?

We want to hear from you!

Do you have a few minutes to participate in a brief online survey?

Microsoft is interested in hearing your feedback so we can continually improve our books and learning resources for you.

To participate in our survey, please visit:

www.microsoft.com/learning/booksurvey/

...and enter this book's ISBN-10 or ISBN-13 number (located above barcode on back cover*). As a thank-you to survey participants in the United States and Canada, each month we'll randomly select five respondents to win one of five $100 gift certificates from a leading online merchant. At the conclusion of the survey, you can enter the drawing by providing your e-mail address, which will be used for prize notification only.

Thanks in advance for your input. Your opinion counts!

* Where to find the ISBN on back cover

ISBN-13: 000-0-0000-0000-0
ISBN-10: 0-0000-0000-0

00000

0 000000 000000

Example only. Each book has unique ISBN.

Microsoft Press

No purchase necessary. Void where prohibited. Open only to residents of the 50 United States (includes District of Columbia) and Canada (void in Quebec). For official rules and entry dates see:

www.microsoft.com/learning/booksurvey/

About the Authors

Sara Froehlich

Sara Froehlich is a contributing writer for *Photoshop Elements Techniques*. She is an instructor at Eclectic Academy at *www.eclecticacademy.com* and LVS Online at *www.lvsonline.com,* where she teaches classes on Adobe Illustrator, Photoshop Elements, and other graphics programs. She is the Photoshop instructor at Digital Art Academy at *www.digitalartacademy.com.*

Over the past five years, she has authored 35 six-week courses in Adobe Photoshop and Photoshop Elements, Adobe Illustrator, Adobe Acrobat, Xara Xtreme, Corel PHOTO-PAINT, Macromedia Dreamweaver, Macromedia Freehand, and Macromedia Fireworks, among others. She also co-authored a Creature House Expression 3 course with Annie Ford. Her Web site, *www.northlite.net*, has more information on her classes, as well as tutorials for Microsoft Expression Design, Adobe Illustrator, and Adobe Photoshop.

Thanks

Many thanks to Sandra Haynes, Rosemary Caperton, Susie Bayers, Juliana Aldous, Nancy Muir, and the whole Microsoft Press crew. Very many thanks to Marc Campbell.

Undying gratitude goes to Tom, my partner and husband of 33 years, for doing everything in his power to let me have writing time. I truly could not have done this without your love and support, and that of our children.

Marc Campbell

Marc Campbell is a technology author, Web designer, and instructor. His popular guides to computer graphics have appeared around the world in eight languages. Among his professional design credentials are the official sites for DC Comics and *MAD* Magazine and service portals for various state governments.